Verses

that

Hurt

Pleasure and Pain

from the

Poemfone Poets

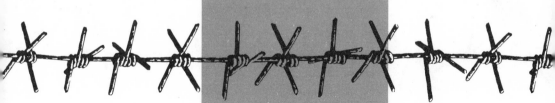

Verses
that
Hurt

Pleasure and Pain
from the
Poemfone Poets

Edited by
JORDAN and AMY TRACHTENBERG

Photographs by
CHRISTIAN LANTRY

Introduction by
TODD COLBY

ST. MARTIN'S PRESS ≋ NEW YORK

A full list of permissions appears on page 212.

VERSES THAT HURT: PLEASURE AND PAIN FROM THE POEMFONE POETS. Copyright © 1996 by Naked Ear
Productions. All photographs copyright © 1996 Christian Lantry except Allen Ginsberg, copyright
© Elsa Dorfman, and Christian Lantry, copyright © Peter Buckingham Photography. All rights
reserved. Printed in the United States of America. No part of this book may be used or reproduced
in any manner whatsoever without written permission except in the case of brief quotations
embodied in critical articles or reviews. For information, address St. Martin's Press, 175 Fifth
Avenue, New York, N.Y. 10010.

Production Editor: David Stanford Burr
Design by Songhee Kim

Library of Congress Cataloging-in-Publication Data

Verses that hurt : pleasure and pain from the poemfone poets / [selected by] Jordan and Amy
    Trachtenberg : photographs by Christian Lantry
            p.   cm.
        ISBN 0-312-15191-8
        1. American poetry—New York (State)—New York. 2. American poetry—New York
    Metropolitan Area. 3. American poetry—20th century. I. Trachtenberg. Jordan.
    II. Trachtenberg. Amy.
    PS549.N5V47   1997
    811'.5408097471—dc21   96-45529
                                                                                CIP

10 9 8 7 6 5 4

Books are available in quantity for promotional or premium use. Write to Director of Special Sales,
St. Martin's Press, 175 Fifth Avenue, New York, N.Y. 10010, for information on discounts and terms,
or call toll-free (800) 221-7945. In New York, call (212) 674-5151 (ext. 645).

For Miriam Trachtenberg

CONTENTS

FOREWORD: FROM POLYESTER TO POETRY

So, it's 1997 and here we are. You and me, me and you . . . plus a few poets, twenty-six to be exact, and of course, the link that brings us all together—this book.

Verses That Hurt is about friendship, music, and poetry. It's about becoming aware, having your eyes stretched wide open, and your mind expanded. It's about love, spirituality, and honesty. It's a gift, it's a mirror, it's a weapon. It's a chapter in the story of how poetry changed my life. So, before you move on to become acquainted with the poets, you should know how we've all arrived at this juncture.

In 1987 I moved from the land of cheese steak to the city that never sleeps. I was fulfilling a dream—albeit not my own—and joining the family business. You see, I'm from a long line of Garmentos. My grandfather and his two sons all worked in the rag trade, and now it was my turn to join the ranks of the fast-tongued polyester pushers that came before me. I was eighteen—too young to drink, but old enough to learn how to show a blouse line. It was official, I had begun my career in Manhattan's notorious Garment Center selling moderately priced missy blouses. My first real achievement was winning the respect of my coworkers and accounts—no easy task for a freshly crowned boss's son. They were prepared to watch me stumble but I wouldn't give them that satisfaction.

A year came and went and New York and the Garment Center were both racing through my veins. After countless hours in a midtown showroom, I had mastered the art of the sell, and it was a rush. Business was booming, units were flying out of the warehouse, and we were all coasting through the eighties. I had made the transformation from snot-nosed punk to proven business man and I was living in the greatest playground on earth, the city of sin, a virtual concrete jungle that stimulated my mind and all of its secret longings. The city made all things seem possible—it titillated my already obsessive love of music and art and quenched my thirst for pop culture, the underground, and, most importantly, the bizarre. Slowly, the same Garment Center that had been my passport to explore my dreams began to feel more and more like a prison. I started to lead a secret life at night, losing the suit and tie for ripped jeans and a ratty T-shirt. I became a regular at downtown venues like CBGB's, the old Knitting Factory, Brownies, The Gas Station, and Tramps, and suddenly it occurred to me—I had never felt more at home.

Enter Lori—literally the girl next door. We had engaged in the usual neighbor stuff—I lent her my corkscrew, she borrowed some sugar, we shot-the-shit in the hallways. Then, one day she hands me a CD and says, "Check this out. A friend of mine from Iowa is the drummer in this band and something tells me it's more your speed than mine." It was a self-titled CD from a band named Drunken Boat. Well, not only did this CD quickly become a favorite but it profoundly affected my life. I became captivated by the band's post-punk, pop-jangle sound and I was entranced by front man Todd Colby's poetic and surreal lyrics. His range of style was astounding—one minute he possessed the softness and innocence of a cushy child, the next minute he would become maniacal and angry, delivering melodic hooks intertwined with twisted images.

> Get off the tractor
> Get on
> The bail
> Pry it off
> The table
> Take my nipple
> Between my fingers
> Big Wheat

> —Drunken Boat, *Tragic Hands*

For months this CD held a distinguished place in my CD player—it was almost always in the spindle. Then one day I read in the *Village Voice* that the band would be playing at the Knitting Factory and I wasn't going to miss it. As it turns out, it was a night of many firsts—the first date with my future wife Amy, the first time I witnessed the crazy antics of Todd Colby, and the first of many times I saw Drunken Boat. Two weeks later I went back for more. The band was playing at CBGB'S and after the show I shyly approached Todd. I told him that he came across to me as a poet just as much as a singer. He retorted that he was a poet and quickly produced a chapbook filled with his poems. I bought his five-dollar handmade book entitled "Fog And Swirl"—a classic Evil Clown publication that is still one of my favorite books to this day. I remember being stunned by his magnetic personality and his genuine friendliness. He took down my address and promised to send me old Drunken Boat tapes and postcards announcing his coming poetry readings, and by God, he kept his word.

Next thing I knew, Amy and I started to hit the poetry circuit, following Todd from cafés to churches, bookstores to parks. From the first reading at the Poetry Project I knew we were in for a wild ride. It wasn't a chore or a bore, it was new, edgy, and captivating. It was all so exciting and fresh—poets speaking, shouting, whispering, and crying their poems as if aiming directly for my ears. Todd and I started talking regularly on the phone and he took great pleasure in exposing me to a host of other poets. And it didn't stop there.

Over the next few months, Todd and I grew closer and closer. We were both heavy into music and we went nuts turning each other on to new sounds. We also shared a love for devilish pranks and while I don't want to reveal too many details, suffice it to say that we tortured many of our friends, and our friends'

friends, with freaky, deranged phone calls. During this time, Todd developed a nasty habit of leaving long rants on my answering machine . . . several times a day. The messages were pure Todd—nonsense fused with poetic beauty—and they took over my machine, leaving little to no room for real messages. Todd was unrelenting—he never missed a day. So I had no choice but to have a sit-down with the madman. I offered to rent a voice mail line where he could rant and rave to his heart's content and other people could call up and hear his insanity, too. I made Todd an offer he couldn't refuse. The deal was simple—he had to change the message everyday or I would stop paying for the line. Hence the birth of the Poemfone. I started printing up catchy postcards with the Poemfone number and a cheesy motto and Todd would throw them out to the crowd during Drunken Boat shows. We scattered them out at all the poetry venues, dropped them in bars, bathrooms, cabs, and bookstores. You name a place and we dropped a card there. And guess who called? The world.

Now, this was cool . . . this was a gas. Todd teased and taunted the callers with poems and monologues and they SPOKE BACK after the beep. Some spewed poems of their own, some offered up their unmitigated critique, some jerked off, and lots and lots of callers were speechless and hung up. CLICK. Soon other poets wanted to rule the line and although Todd had become a Poemfone addict, he agreed to share the delight of it all with his comrades in words. We decided that Todd would host the line for the first three days of every month and then pass it off to a different poet. (This three-day stint, now a Poemfone tradition, is commonly referred to as the Todd Colby Buffer Zone.) We came up with two golden rules: the poets had to commit to hosting the line for the entire month and they had to promise to record a new poem on the line daily. It was a great challenge to the poets and a great opportunity too for the callers to become familiar with a range of work from one poet. It was unreal. Soon we started getting calls from other states, then other countries. And all the while I was at home recording both ends of the line. We were creating controlled chaos, living art, poetic communication. We had started an intricate chain of action and reaction.

The next few months raced by. . . . In September, Wanda Phipps became the second Poemfone poet and Amy and I tied the knot. Todd, my only groomsman to forget to wear underwear, stood under my Chuppa during our wedding ceremony and read the following poem:

Love Is a Many Splendoured Thing

Some say love is as soft as an easy chair
on which a cranked-up weasel sits snapping at your neck.

I'm not so sure about that, what I do know is that
this day is unlike any other day
but then, all the days will eventually blend into one day
and that day is RIGHT NOW
and THIS day will be featured in your memory
for years to come.

What we are about to witness is a gas.
It's amusing in the true sense of the word "amusing"
in other words, "to be conducted by a muse."
To be inspired on the wedding of friends is no small feat.
I feel damaged and dimpled.
My own exploits in the field of love
so failing at times, so thick in its achievements
so tired
sometimes
of the word "love."

There's something beyond that.
there's a whiplash, smack dab, bonus point
bond that comes from suffering together.

The world is very frightening in 1994.
I'm scared. I'm running out of gas.
I'm starting to bob and weave.
I believe I've lost my course.

But love comes in so many fabulous forms!
I'm a child in the face of love!
I fawn and purr in the face of love!
I laugh and gasp in the face of love!
Love is the most fabulous thing in the universe!
Love is the reason we all got out of bed this morning.
For love! For love! For lovely love!
For the ever present danger of it all ending!
For the chance Amy and Jordy are taking!
For there never to be uttered again the words
"Did you get a tux yet?"
"Did you really get a single-breasted jacket?"
"Did you write the poem yet?"

Soon we'll go on with our lives
and Amy and Jordy will go on with theirs.
And one day, not too long from now,
Jordy will pitter-patter across the floor

in his fleece-lined slippers
and look Amy straight in the eyes
and they will be immobilized by the sudden
mutual realization that they are blessed by
the love of so many friends.

They will appear,
as they sit on the floor of their
sprawling loft,
to be two deer caught in the headlights of an oncoming truck.
They will shudder as though a defensive lineman
had thrown a cooler full of iced Gatorade on their backs.

They will laugh and remember this day.

Needless to say, our guests were left dazzled and confused and I can assure you the cantor was stunned. My honeymoon marked my first absence from the daily ins and outs of the Poemfone but from the moment I landed back in New York I reconnected. (I remember calling in from the baggage claim at Kennedy to hear the smooth sounds of Shannon Ketch—Mr. October.) A month at a time I came to appreciate and admire a new poet: Ms. Blackman left me speechless with her pop culture incitements; M. Doughty touched me with his cool passion; and in January the elastic-tongued Edwin Torres left me speechless. By April we had booked the line through the end of the year and the lineup was killer.

Several times a day I would call in from work—it became my three-minute escape. Okay, I admit it. I, too, had become a Poemfone junkie, and I soon discovered that I wasn't alone. Callers were leaving declarations of Poemfone love in their messages. We had all become a part of some poetic cult and Todd and I were loving every minute of it. And then one day while at work, I had a revelation. I was on the phone with a blouse buyer from down south. She was gnawing on my ass over a shipment that was a week late. You would have thought that the world was coming to an end over late polyester. Nauseous, I hung up the phone wondering how the fuck was I going to get out of women's wear hell. Then, ZAP, it hit me like a white light. I knew I had to make a Poemfone CD. I imagined watching each poet freak freely in a recording studio, some backed by bands, some a capella. And hey, maybe I could even make use of those bizarre Poemfone responses I'd been recording all year. I went home that night and laid out my inspired plan to Amy.

After eight years of ups and downs in the Garment Center, I was finally ready to walk away forever. My friends and family were shocked yet supportive and all asked me if I knew what I was doing. The truth of the matter was I didn't. But I had a vision and I wasn't going to let anything get in my way. On April Fool's Day 1995, I booked recording time at Studio Twist and began to chase my own dream. This was what I really wanted to be doing with my life—I was making something I believed in, art. During the course of a month the CD came to life and before I even had a tape I was "shopping" the project around and a surprising number of labels were interested in taking it. I was ecstatic. Everything suddenly made sense. I was using the same sales skills I had honed selling schmata's and I was feeding my creative side.

After a fair amount of obsessing, I made the decision to put the CD out through Tomato Records. Kevin Eggers, the owner of the label, believed in this project wholeheartedly. He showed me his catalog of artists whom he had worked with and produced in the past and it was an eclectic and impressive list, chock-full of legends from the late Townes Van Zandt to John Lee Hooker, Albert King, and Doc Watson. He even did a few spoken-word records with the great Dick Gregory. More importantly, Tomato Records had Warner Bros. distribution, which meant that when the Poemfone CD was released it would hit music stores in a big way. The deal was looking very good and then it just got better. Kevin believed in me. He recognized my vision and enthusiasm and knew that I wanted to get in, to learn, to make things happen. He offered me a job as his label manger and director of A&R. Here it was, in front of me, my dream job. I had found my way into the music business.

So, on April 9, 1996, the critically acclaimed *Poemfone: New Word Order* made it's way into the world. With this first dream coming to fruition I realized that I couldn't stop striving, which brings us to this book. What you have here represents two years of the Poemfone, in all its poetic glory. Now, if I were you, and I know I'm not, I would take the chance and read this book aloud. Read it to your friends, offend your loved ones, woo a mate, let your voice ring out. Flick your tongue like serpent, pop your lips like a cannon, shoot the words from your throat like sparks from your soul. Hear the words resonate. 'Cause I've learned from experience that if you bite into the words, they're sure to bite you back.

—Jordan N. Trachtenberg
New York City
1996

INTRODUCTION

What you are holding in your hands right now is a book. Not a telephone receiver, which is how most of the poems in this collection were first transmitted. Now they're on the page again, which means we've made the leap from spoken word to written word in less than two years. Personally, I still think it's fantastic to be able to pick up the phone on some sleepless rainy night and hear a poem read by the poet who wrote it. It was Frank O'Hara, that ecstatic New York poet, who said he could just as easily pick up the phone as write a poem. I agree, there's room for both. Poemfone, in its own small way, has enabled poetry to become a part of the fabric of our lives. Where else can you hear a poem and leave a message at the beep? Now, when you need a poetry fix you can also pop in a CD *(Poemfone: New Word Order)*, boot up your computer (www.nakedear.com), or crack open a book and flow down a river of words. Poetry SHOULD be everywhere and slowly but surely it's infiltrating our lives. We are glad to be the instruments of this infiltration.

The idea of transmitting poetry over phone lines isn't anything new really. We just took the idea and updated it with cutting edge technology, also known as, ahem, voice mail. The first time poetry versified the phone lines was way back in 1968 when John Giorno had the marvelous idea of assembling thirteen poets who each read twelve poems onto an old analog reel-to-reel tape recorder. The poems and poets were changed everyday. So, if you called several times in one day you'd most likely hear a different poem by that poet each time you called. All this was housed and financed by the Architectural League on East Sixty-fifth Street in Manhattan. The participants in Dial-a-Poem (as it was dubbed) are worth mentioning: Allen Ginsberg, David Henderson, Anne Waldman, Lewis Warsh, Ron Padgett, Bill Berkson, William Burroughs, Taylor Mead, John Perreault, Ed Sanders, Peter Schjeldahl, and Emmit Williams. That's quite a list, huh? Well, Dial-a-Poem went along smoothly until some obscenity charges were brought against the line, and the whole thing had to be shut down. Many of the readings still exist on records and CDs that John Giorno still releases on his Dial-a-Poem record label. They are worth having, believe me.

There are plenty of examples of the spreading of one art form or another through popular mediums. There are all those wonderful Russian Constructivist posters, Happenings from the folks who brought us Fluxus, Dr. Alphabet's public poetry gatherings on football fields and street corners, Forty-second Street marquees, Dada cabaret antics, and various forms of street theater, need I go on? Essentially what all these movements were trying to do was expand the playing field called "ART." By making the field bigger they gave us all more room to frolic. They pushed art right out of the dusty museums and smack dab into our lives. Our REAL day-to-day lives, and that's no small feat. Art *should* be a part of our lives, not something reserved merely for special occasions—that sounds too much like church to me. Art should fit into our lives like a warm meal, or a smack on the back of the head, or a bad night on a strange new drug, or a lover's kiss. That's why I think Poemfone, in its own humble way, has continued the tradition of populist rebellion. Oh yeah, we're rebels, look out!

The country-simple concept behind the Poemfone is to make spoken word available over the phone for free. I like to think of it as using poetry to illuminate the technological void. If you need a poem you pick up the phone, and if the poem sucks you hang up, and if it's good you can explain the bliss of their words at the beep. Voice mail is the tool! It's an all-new free-form grandstand for poets and callers-in alike. Oh those callers! Those message mongers dialing from bedrooms, boardrooms, asylums, and wherever else people have managed to install phones or point satellite dishes. They are the juice behind the phone. We set it up and they called. They left their daily opuses, jittery critiques, bold musings, wild rants, and cool verbal sex fidgets. It's like dragging one of those huge fishing nets across a digital sea. You too can leave a message at the end of the poem. You can now put this book down and make a quick call to (212) 631-4234. You must respond immediately. It's all about your response. Well, that and the poetry.

Would Walt Whitman have participated in the Poemfone? Gertrude Stein? Arthur Rimbaud? Langston Hughes? Djuna Barnes? Emily Dickinson? Mina Loy? Sappho? William Blake? You Betcha! Something tells me that if they were alive now they'd be doing the Fone. Why? Writers have always used the tools of their time to spread the word. Oh yeah, there were probably holdouts and grumblers when Guttenberg's Press was booted up, and when Archilochus first strummed his lyre and shouted "Iambic Pentameter!" over the Cycladic islands, I'm sure there were some folks growling, "Oh no, not HIM again!"

That such well-established poets as Allen Ginsberg, John Giorno, Bob Holman, and Penny Arcade chose to participate in this anthology gives me great hope in bridging the generation gap that seems to have occurred in certain literary circles. These are some of the people who helped shape us as writers. They are our teachers, our role models, our friends. Certainly they are part of that group of poets who made the playing field bigger for us all. It is a thrill and honor to have them appear side by side with so many fresh young voices. There is hope.

Gertrude Stein said, "When poetry really began it practically included everything." I believe she was right. This anthology certainly illustrates that fact. There is something for everyone here. The variety is simply astounding: There's Penny Arcade's hot wall of sound, Tish Benson's fractured smooth molasses, Nicole Blackman's prickly pear prosody, David Cameron's surreal bear cub brew, Xavier Cavazos's silky smooth musical musings, my own caffeinated pleasures, Matthew Courtney's multiple voiced game-show-host-on-poetry vibe, M. Doughty's Sam Spade hip-hop, Kathy Ebel's soft Eartha Kitt explosions, Anne Elliott's supercharged Gregorian rants, Janice Earlbaum's wicked revelations,

Allen Ginsberg's ecstatic wise music, John Giorno's perfpo purity, John S. Hall's urban neurotic hilarity, Bob Holman's electro-dynamic verse, Christian X. Hunter's crazy calm observations, Shannon Ketch's midwest meets New York surrealismo, Bobby Miller's fierce yet gentle ravings, Wanda Phipps's slithery sound scapes, Lee Ranaldo's hell-dipped sweetness, Shut-Up Shelley's provocative verbal slashings, Hal Sirowitz's wacky profundities, Sparrow's zen absurdities, Spiro's indignant tongue lashings, Edwin Torres's wildcat Dada tenderness, and Emily XYZ's elegant thunder. Whew, see what I mean about variety? Hey, don't believe me, read them for yourself.

Good poetry should get at the heart via the ear, as if warm olive oil were being poured down your ear canal. It should also rattle you, rough you up, calm you down, jostle and surprise you. It should clench your throat tight as a fist but it should also seduce you, even turn you on, if need be. The poetry in this anthology may be a little harsh at times but even in its harshness it's still expressing the joy of existence. Even the angry poems are tempered with precision, which is what makes them so lethal. It's always apparent when a poet is testing herself, testing you, tweaking your mental nipples until you are moved. If you feel your blood surging and your pulse quicken chances are you're either reading a great poem or spending wonderful time with a lover.

Writing is the transference of energy from one person to another. The energy in this book is big, beautiful, and sometimes downright ugly, but that's okay because energy can be anything poetry wants it to be. A lot of the energy in this anthology comes from various musical forms. Thumb through this tome and you'll see elements of hip-hop, classical, punk, jazz, trip-hop, industrial slamcore . . . oh yeah, it's all here. These are mere labels, the point is that the cross-pollination of music and poetry (which really began as one) is our supergrow lawn food. Good poetry is about being open to the infinite possibilities amid so many artificial limitations. In order for poetry to survive (or any living organism for that matter) it must learn to adapt to a changing environment. We are under constant attack by silly and horrible forces that would rather have us watch a movie of the week than enjoy a poem. Competing with these distractions is no small feat—being heard above the din of clanging televisions, sirens, and bombs calls for desperate measures. Those measures are not in short supply in this book. Can you hear me?

St. Martin's Press should be applauded for publishing this anthology but I must also make a plug here for small press poetry. Buy it. Go down to your local bookstore and demand it. Many of the poets in this anthology (including myself) have books that are published by small presses. I would suggest that you start by perhaps contacting Small Press Distribution in Berkeley, California, and asking them for a catalogue. They have the most complete collection of independently produced literature in the country. You know, for some reason, everyone seems to be listening but very few are actually reading or buying— change that now—it's important that small presses stay alive, so support them.

So, take this book as a challenge—to start your own Poemfone (it only costs about ten bucks a month to rent a voice mail line—only don't call it Poemfone, that's us), your own mimeo press, fanzine, poemzine, Internet home page assaults, posters, broadsides—do anything just "make it new" as Ezra Pound would say—invent new forms, bring fresh air to poetry at every possible opportunity, otherwise what's the point?

See you on the Fone—

—Todd Colby
New York City
1996

"Reality" is the only word in the language that should always be used in quotes.

Penny
Arcade

Manifesto

Here is my personal message to all of you
careerist, slime bucket, fame seeking, sychophantic,
weakworded, same voiced, gladhanding, asskissing,
backstabbing, envying, self serving assholes
who are littering the downtown scene in ever increasing
numbers while you choke the creativity out of yourselves as
you turnoff thousands of potential power of the word
lovers by the oxygen you use up on the performing stages of
New York City while you make your dullwitted stab toward
your myopic fantasy of love, admiration, approval, sex and
immortality which you think your 10 minutes of standing in
front of a crowd that has long stopped listening to you will
confer on your sorry asses.

Stop practicing in public
memorizing your poem won't make up
for it being shitty and empty in the first place.
your friends in the poetry scene
will not tell you that you suck
they are happy you suck
because they are as competitive as you are
they'll keep telling you how great you are as long as you
return the favor or until they feel they are more successful
than you
stop whining about not being invited to read at the St Mark's
Poetry Project on New Years Day
it's a benefit
not a career move.
Stop whining about what time
yer given to read on New Years Day
9 out of 10 times you don't even deserve to be reading there.
Stop telling us that you will
kill yourself if you don't become famous
it is of no interest to us
as a matter of fact
I want you to kill yourself
if that's what it takes to get you
to stop performing in public
and please. . . . .

Don't leave a note.
You have to be willing to be bad for 20 years to be great
and there's no guarantee you will be
Unless you have an intimate relationship with someone the
people who rush to congratulate you as you come offstage
are even more desperate than you are
Anyone can kill on stage for six minutes
the measure is can you kill for 3 hours?
The only thing of value anyone has to offer
is their uniqueness
and individuality
no matter who you are or what you do.
Live your life.
Notice what you are really thinking about
Write about that.
Show us what you don't want anyone to see.
Remember that while art can be product
product can never be art
Take a real risk just once.
Judge other artists by the quality of their work
not by how nice they are to you.
Read. Listen.
Read. Listen.
Read. Listen.
Stop being part of the most illiterate, unread group of poseurs
in the long history of poseurs in art.
Stop confusing performance poetry with:
Saturday Night Live
Sesame Street
having a good time
a Tupperware party
hanging out with yer friends
Wheel of Fortune
Jeopardy!
your senior prom
The Brady Bunch

No Mona Lisa (for Henry Everingham)

I am magnum mouthed
honey snatched
my flavor changes constantly
No Mona Lisa
I stroll like a sailor
bullets pass thru me and I keep moving.
No Mona Lisa
I don't hang around
but if I have it for you
you are lucky
you can take it to the track
you can take it to the bank
you can deposit it
No Mona Lisa
No sidelong glance
no rolling eye
supposition, preposition
have no place in my communication.
When I talk
you know exactly what I mean.
Mona Lisa has no mouth,
no cunt,
she stops at the waist.
I hate that bitch!
My head turns from side to side
My brain, mouth and cunt all work.
No Mona Lisa
I can't be displayed, restored
or evaluated.
No Mona Lisa
I read the writing on the wall behind me.
No Mona Lisa
I don't preview.
No Mona Lisa
No auction.
No rebate.
No Mona Lisa
I don't discount, price down or go on sale.
No Mona Lisa

5

When I'm in love I stay wet all the time!
Mona Lisa has no mouth, no cunt, she stops at the waist.
I hate that bitch!
No Mona Lisa
No side long manipulation.
I never had a father.
I never learned how to be that kind of whore.
You need a daddy to practice that kind of stalking.
You need a daddy.
I never apprenticed to my mother.
I wasn't well for that center of attention and protection.
I was nobody's angel.
nobody's princess.
nobody's baby.
I grew wild, uncultivated, ungroomed, unprotected,
to a position of power
I'm a loner. You are lucky.
I know what you want, when you want it, how you want it.
I deliver without a sermon.
My religion has no pope, no choir, no hope
I'm a loner. You are lucky.
No Mona Lisa
I never learned how to simmer contentedly.
I boil over continuously.
Hot sweet syrup between my legs
When I'm in love I stay wet all the time!
No Mona Lisa
I cannot be catalogued or dissertated
I cannot be viewed from a different angle,
a different perspective.
I cannot be seen in a different light.
Mona Lisa has no mouth! No cunt! She stops at the waist!
I hate that bitch!
Mona Lisa sits.
I stand
two lightening bolts in my fists
a crescent moon over my cunt.
No Mona Lisa
I cannot be swayed, rehung or framed.
I don't need special lights, special glass
or a smoke free environment.
No Mona Lisa
No refracted light, no insurance.
I am no collector's item.

no curator's pet.
I am no one's voyeur, no one's witness.
I cannot be replicated, calendared
or placed on coffee mugs.
No Mona Lisa
I am 3D
You can touch me.
I touch back.
I bite back, spit back, talk back.
No Mona Lisa
No Gioconda smile
No Mona Lisa
I tell you the truth.
I am ruthless.
You are lucky.

Haiku (for Todd Colby)

I thought you were Kurt Cobain
but then he died and you were still around.

Consider the Discourse

There are people with black skin.
There are people with red skin.
There are people with white skin.
There are people with brown skin.
There are people with olive sin.
There are people with yellow skin.
That's it.
Some are assholes.
Some aren't.

CONSIDER THE DISCOURSE FORMALLY CLOSED.

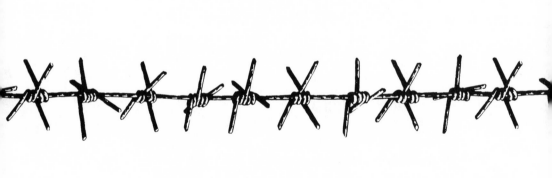

Tish
Benson

Sweet Obsession

Itsa about
green n spring
rice n beans
cornbread & cold cold buttermilk
iced down beer
in 101 degrees

here me out!!!

No potpourri
could smell
as good as you

Hersheys
Mars
&
Godiva
 all
been tryin
to emulate yo sweetness

they havent gotten close

Think about it:
If toilets were
animate
yours would
      grin
         real loud baby

& further
u make my insides
feel like a
big bowl
of spicy gumbo
when
icecicles
      hang
         from the rooftop.

in tha a.m.

i
wake up in tha mornin
with yo scent on my tongue   through my lungs

sayin: come on with it sweet meat
                       tha gettin don't get
             mo gooder than at this
                  point of tha day . . .
          understand me!
        this time i'll be scooby doo
             u be tha snack . . .

am i on to something here?
i say we played foreplay   all nite long

skied cross brooklyn bridge

        floatin on layers of lotus petals

              drinkin mint tea rivers

rollin in fruit juice

        goin ahh yeah mmmmhuh wellallrightbaby . . .

ya smile tells me i'm on ta somethin here

times a wastin   we wastin time
come a little closer
why dontcha

cuz wide open spaces
is for country roads

        its plenty of leg room
where we jettin
             ahhhammmmyeahhhhhh

i think we're on to somethin here

IT IS WHAT IT IS . . . & then some

My man strums his own
ez on tha bones
symphony
& his phunk don't stank

When he sends
lightnin bolts
through my
pelvic region
tha neighbors
bang on tha walls

"YALL TURN THAT MUSIC DOWN"

see scatin
aint in their
repotoire
of today
sounds

I smile up to him
even when i'm drivin
and he grins right on back
cause he know he tha man

"YEAH BABY U THA MAN ALRIGHT. U THA MAN"

His sweat glistens
like molten bronze
I taste his textures
knowin
his is tha best meal on this planet
& his phunk don't stank

I'ma write a poem
dedicated to his
hoochie-coo
just as soon as we
come on down.

trippin

boredom is the hoodoo drug of the masses
they are caught up in a monotone cycle
it meanders from umbilical chord to sidewalks
gray crusty and filled inbetween with halfs and wholes but not
completes
minds are corrupted to this degree too
but angles are always a different color
green is the fatback that transcends racial indifference
jim jones was hip to this phenomenon
others O.D. on electronic mind altering devices
soon space travel and consteller pastlives will take over as
americas favorite pastimes
look for changes thru large doses of intravenous herbal remedies
all types of passing can also create metamorphistic realities

HOW NOW WHITE COW?

U BE DOIN IT
(To tha brotha who made livers quiver at tha chrismas party)

MMMMMMMMMMMMMMMMMMmmmmmmmmmmmmmmmmmmmmmmmmm
mmmmmmmmmmmmmmmmmmmmmmmmmm

did u sling it

                        pelvic thrust

middrift YayA

        tha groovy
        moovy   nitty gritty
                Grind

tha shimmy shimmy   shake shake

            tha woO-WOo-Woo HooChIE Coo

boopdeboop
            deBOOPde bEE bOPdeBoPdeBop da Bang bANG

        naa nanana naaa nanana nana na nananananaaaaaaaa

WORK IT BABY WORK IT

yes   u slung it
                                like Hank did his bat
            like Ali did his gloves
                                like Althea did her racket
            like Basquiat did his paintbrush

tha walls started sweatin

                    tha chairs had ta hole on to they legs

tha tablecloths were switchin off tha tables

                    tha floor started clappin
                        &

tha dj went: **PARTY OVAH THERE PARTY RIGHT THERE!!!**
lookin at u only at u

All because u whipped it

like b.b. do to tha blues

like booga do to loo

like mr. leos do to bar-b-que

like jane cortez do to a poem
&
afta u slung it
afta u popped that thang
afta u whipped it
afta all tha ladies in tha
house
said:
OWWW!!! OW OW OWWWWWW!!!

afta captain twobob cut tha motor off
cuz u waz rockin tha boat. . . .

u jes smiled

cuz u know

u be doin it

Nicole
Blackman

You Will

You will smile at me between courses at dinner.
You will stroke your ankle against mine when I'm discussing politics with the
    family.
You will lick away the last traces of dessert from your mouth and never take
    your eyes off me.
You will ask if I know what you're thinking and I will just breathe silently.
You will caress my wrists in the kitchen as I rinse the glasses in warm water.
You will stand behind me, your breath warm on my neck, my ears.
You will slip out when the others go into the living room for coffee and I
    will follow you.
You will clasp me in the yard underneath a tree, with fall air falling on us.
You will sweep in my trembles and brush in my heartbeat.
You will sniff hungrily at me and slide your hands under my sweater, blouse,
    bra to skin and me.
You will gather me in to you and your mouth will wet and bite me like fruit.
You will murmur and moan and pull me pull me pull me to you under the
    night sky.
You will shift me down to the cold grass and I will never once think that this
    is wrong, that I am your sister and you cannot have me this way.
You will not utter a word and when you are done you will lay beside me
    and wrap me in a deep blanket of stars.

Rockaway

fuck him.
get it over with.
you need a place to stay tonight.

you don't really smoke but you ask for a cigarette.
ask for another.
realize you're chainsmoking
so you'll have something to do.
anything to keep from talking to this guy.

wonder why car lighters never work.
look for matches.
realize other people smoke
to keep their hands from shaking.
but yours are twitching hard.

focus hard on the radio.
listen to air supply sing "all out of love"
and smirk because it's so stupid.
realize your eyes are tearing
because it's so beautiful.
god, your nerves are shot.

remember how a friend said he hated blowjobs
because they made women subservient
you said he was crazy because a woman is never
more powerful than when she has
a man's jewels in her mouth.

wonder why they call them blowjobs.
blowing has nothing to do with it.

look at him and wish you weren't here.
realize this was a mistake and swallow hard.
touch his arm to comfort yourself.
see the track marks for the first time.
wish you hadn't fucked him.
wish you'd left the party when you said you would.
sex in cars always makes you feel tired.

drop the cigarette and realize
you smoked it down to the filter.
watch it hit the asphalt
and see it roll away.
keep watching
until the orange glow fades.

settle in against the vinyl
for a long night.

Iris

Iris is writing a poem while I read the paper at her apartment.
she blows a cigarette ash right into her shoe.
it doesn't seem to bother her.

I read the poem later and it doesn't make much sense.
then again, neither does she.
it's Sunday and I'm at her place again.

she plays Strauss and techno on the stereo
as people drop in on her all day long.
it's just that kind of place.
friends stop in and stay for dinner.
her roommate is dying but we don't talk about it.

(she's the one who fixes me when I'm falling apart
—stitches me back together with nicotine and tea)

she's the kind of girl who can make a dress
out of a garbage bag.
she always somehow looks better than I ever will.
there's a lot of drag queen in her.

I lend her books and give her CDs.
we borrow pens and money from each other's bags.
we're beyond the permission phase.

she's not dating anyone now.
she gets crushes on guys and girls but nothing happens.

she travels to places I've only seen in magazines.
she's got friends with no last names.
you can't take a bad picture of her.
she falls out of bed and somehow looks glamorous.
I paint her toenails backstage before a show.
she's so pretty when she smiles.

we can finish each other's sentences.
she laughs a lot.

there's something wrong with her
but she won't say what it is.

she's the only friend who hasn't turned on me yet.
but she will.
they always do.

Break

It will come on a cold street corner
after a lovely dinner,
the kind of evening that feels like
an American Express commercial,
where you are young and happy;
the kind that makes you feel
lucky to be alive and 24
with a man who thinks you are
beautiful and smart and funny
and worth his time and words.

It will be quick.

It will begin with him stopping you
and saying he needs to talk.
You'll gasp for breath
as you wonder what it is that you did.

It will hurt less if you say it fast,
you'll tell him.
But when he speaks it will be graceless,
ineloquent,
with sentences full of only dry words.

He will say it is him and not you.
He will say how sorry he is,
that you don't deserve this,
that he wishes this all came
at a different time in his life.

He will say that he wants to be friends.

He will finally notice how silent you are,
how much you are in pain.
Your hands will twitch
as you button your coat
against the cold.
You'll bite your lip hard
when the tears come.

The slush on the sidewalk will prevent you from making a clean getaway.

Us

There are so many of us in New York, you know.
We're the ones in bed early, with mud masks on our face
and dozens of unused candles around the room.

Hypnotized, we dive into potato chip bags
and keep eating until Ted Koppel's finished talking about
whatever he's talking about.

Birthdays aren't a big deal.
We try not to make a fuss because every year
we get closer to 30,
closer to not having, never having
the husband and baby
we swore we'd have by now.

We organize our closets,
make pesto,
hem skirts,
keep a journal
and read—a lot.
We have rented every goddamn movie at Blockbuster.

We walk by Baby Gap
and get a pain in our chest.

We start looking at our best friends and think,
hey, why not
—at least I know what she likes in bed.

We know how to make really good chili
but it always tastes funny when we eat it alone.

We sneeze and there is no one to bless us.

The hardest part is the music,
the songs that pour out of elevators and taxis,
with voices that crawl between our ears and say
"This one's about you, babe.
This one's all about you."

David
Cameron

Hello all you dialectical

nimrods
captain january here
  booming through the
  subcontexts in my
  underwear
  —what was he doing
  in your underwear?—
So I ate him.
Did you notice
there's a diphthong in your
  name now? Better
  that than getting up
at 6:30 in the A.M.
to hear the clock bark
and the light pour
into the room
—You think you've got goldfish?
I've got goldfish like
you've never seen
With their own
  printing press
and red army ants
working beneath
to print sans-
  copywright editions
  of Mao's good
  book
Oh it's like sex
  —pouring over the
  illustrations to
  Dante's *Divine Comedy*—
—It's so good
  I can brush my
  teeth with it
and expects sparks to fly
and flocks of seagulls
to come spitting out of
  my gums

I've figured it out
It's gonna be in this
  half of the
century
  who can go fastiest
  who will really earn
  the title
go-getter feisty
  speed guy
Hey you the speed-
  neediest
with the knitted vest
and the KANGOL cap
or you gold tooth
  momma's boy
Don't think that
  I don't know
that McDonald's is
  the new proprietor
  of the reversification
  of America
—Yo I just ate
  the Walt Whitman
Happy Meal
With the deathbed
  edition of
Leafs of Grass
  on the box
And inside are
  stand alone plastic
figures
of Walt laying down
  between the bride
& groom
—Collect them all!

Ode: My Barber's Breath

My barber's breath
    is atrocious
His teeth are barely stubs, disintegrated, retracting,
and the food that is between what remains of them
    has been there since I first walked into his shop
    two years ago, and it is paste now, and
    it was paste then, so maybe before . . .
In the corners of his eyes remains deposited from at least several nights
    of sleep
    an unmoved, yellow crust
But he has the softest hands
His hands are possessed with the touch of
those medieval saints and near saints possessed by jesus
or by his words
or by his sight or those
who spoke with him
and followed his commandments
who had a continuing vision of the rock rolling back
of the ghost   who were touched   who felt the flat palm of the
    virgin mother
resting momentarily on the tops of their skulls

But he is not cutting the rosetta stone
into my scalp
or the deep sea scrolls thank god no
He has craft and his scissors cut hair
or nothing   snip rapidly awaiting instruction
cut into the sound into the air around my ears
and there is a string of drool
descending from his lip I cannot
understand more than half of what he is saying
we invariably have the same
conversation *kids today/terrible, terrible*
no respec/terrible
His language   it is somewhere between italian
and incomprehensible   I imagine
half of his meaning is rolling wet and shiny
over his lip   sticking to his chin where
he does not wipe it away

There is a spot of white puss
        in each corner of his mouth
But he is sweet and gentle
and *a little more here?*
and *a little shorter?*
and the breath that crawls out of his mouth on all fours like a starving dog
        is atrocious
and the only saving graces he has are the only ones
he needs
his light touch, his skill as a barber,
his fingernails
are clean

Verbatim: Myrna Tinoco

        I never had my
        clothes on when I was
        a little girl   I mooned
        my dad once, I think
        when I was six I
        don't really remember
        why

this girl hit me with a rock in my eye
when I was six   we were playing
catch but we didn't have a ball
we were playing catch with a rock and

it hit me   in the eye   cause I
couldn't   catch

        who plays catch
        with a rock

Oh how sad I'll be

when I'm an old man
    and can't jump around my apartment
  to all those funky
        guitar   riffs

  Someone
           please tell me
           old men can jump
      Tell me there is a secret society
                of mad moon jumpers
    who have abandoned this planet
for a thinner atmosphere
and less
      gravitational bring-
            down

Tell me there are
old men
floating
      across and above
      the moon's surface, singing

    We don't need no hundred dollar sneakers
    Alls I need is a bigger pair of speakers!

XXV

You put the universe under your thumb
You bitch! The mood has been torn apart by your cruel donuts.
In order to be the only one with your teeth in the jujubes
Each day you turned your heart into a rattlesnake.
Your eyes light up like a tea shop
You stamp your mark into a river of plum tea
And if the pretty boys don't publish your invitations
You'll leave them with the mark of the prune
And they'll never know the beauty of your boot.

Coffee maker, you shit in my cream!
Trumpet player, you drink up the blood of the world.
Haven't you walked anywhere? how could you not
Have seen in car windows the reflections of your hair?
The ugliness of your hairdo, which you believe ingenious
Has never gotten you pushed off a dock
But like nature, deserves to be hidden in a cave.
From you I smell fresh breath o woman! o queen of fishing in the rain.
—From you, vile animal fall the wages of tragedy!
What big teeth you have! How subtle your idiocy!

Falsely translated from Baudelaire's poem "Tu mettrais l'univers entier dans ta ruelle"
from *Les Fleurs Du Mal.*

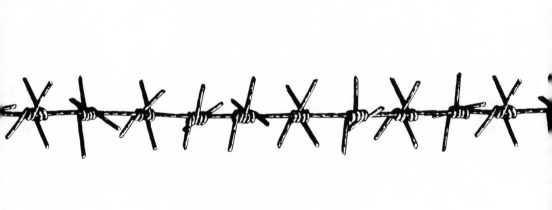

Xavier
Cavazos

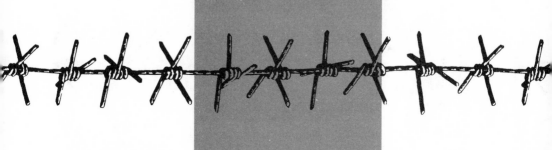

Today

I almost slipped into your cup of coffee
The aroma was sweet   the beans so dark
Who could blame me for walking on the rim
Dipping my pinky from time to time
Taking such chances in testing the temperatures
I only did well   in catching myself in time
Catching myself before my breath stank
Like milk and beans   before
The temperature changes everything to liquid
Before   my cum smelled like coffee

Manteca

Crisco never felt like it felt when
Anna Marie put it on me
The *manteca* would just melt in
Her hands   like summer
I never understood why that never happened
When mom put it on

My hair needed alot &
Anna Marie knew it
Knew how to squeeze the lard just
Right between each hair &
The hair after
Knew how to comb it just right
With her thin fingers

Knew just right
How to make a boy worship a can

Chinatown

i walk down the streets of the lower east side
bowery   red light   cross street   yellow light
beautiful chinese got me all mixed up fall down on my knees
now i'm playing nick nack patty wack on the back
of some crackerjack who stabbed his girl jill
ran down the hill to buy crack from freaked out phil
who moved out here from the west coast   talkin'
his shit was the most   but damn that white boy looked like a ghost
or did someone say de la dana burnt toast
but i pick up the beat as i walk down the street into
some spanish harlem hell hole   talkin' this & that &
what about that cat who used to live on the corner of 106th &
lenox   playin' his horn like a train for a mile or a
miles davis coltrane runnin' down the track like
some freaked out junky who took her life over some 5
dollar bet or ten dollar hit   now she's playin'
nick nack patty wack on her own back
bent up like some bad dog packed up in the ground
but i almost lose my cool when some puerto rican fool
steps up to me & starts to drool 'bout me lookin' so white
so why don't i get out of sight   so i take a step back &
drop a stupid mira mira me no speak puerto rican
but i'm completely mexican rhyme on him like he was dime
so the fool doesn't even take time to say he's sorry
just splits like a dark paul tsongas or a slick jimmy smits
so now i'm standin' around midtown tryin' to get downtown
to get back to the streets that know my beats or
at least i got some warm sheets waitin' with me
with maria or natalia   o puerto rican my heart
natalia bonilla   thank you & good night

Sucking

Rush Limbaugh   you are Mexican Salsa
On ice cream
Soy sauce on cereal

My mother's hospital bed
After my birth
A man's penis in a boy's mouth
Hot air on New York streets
The urine so thick you think it's a shake
Limbaugh   you are all of this
A straw in rotten cum

Note to Miss Gonzalez from Mrs. Goodrich

Pick up the following: Asparagus
                         Spinach
                         Beets
                         Cotton
                         & Apples

No problem Doña
I picked the Asparagus while the April weather
Chilled my hands   only able to cut one at a time
By the end of the day I had two thousand

No problem Doña
I picked the Spinach when the leaves were wet &
Would wrap around my knees
By noon not even my lunch was dry

No problem Doña
I picked the Beets   it was three in the morning
While I was thinning the plants   trying to keep good
Posture while you were still dreaming

No problem Doña
I picked the Cotton when the weather was hot &
White & my hands turned the crop red with every prick
While you just turned your head

No problem Doña
I picked the Apples for a dollar a barrel
I walked miles up & down   going nowhere
I could've walked to Mexico

No problem Doña
The D'Agostino is just down the road

Letter to Gil from White Center

Gil the Seattle sky is light tonight & clouds are heavy
As usual   it's been storming all week here & i see
That the weather in New York is doing the same
CNN is great   it allows you to never go outside
Ted Turner should run for president   everybody gets to vote
From their television sets   i think he would win
Unless of course he's Jewish or Mexican &
You are Fleishman & i am Cavazos
& the best either of us could ever hope for are good
University jobs   maybe Brooklyn college
I hear Ginsberg teaches there   what do you think Joshua
From the Old Testament   i mean the Torah
No disrespect intended would say about that
Would he would drop down like rain around Noah's
Boat & pronounce himself a ghost
Or would he stand at the plank end of his own death &
Beg for his sons circumcision   would he even
Acknowledge Christ before the last gulp of air &
Water would fill his throat & name his lung
Mathew   Ruth
Samuel   Luke
Daniel   John
You see Gil we keep coming back to the same point &
Argument   Christ is Jewish & Jewish is
Christ   & i   & we   & you see no word bends straight here
Coney Island & Crown Heights
Red Hook   the Bronx
New Jersey & N.Y.U.
God is spirit Gil   God is spirit
In spirit   in us
Light

Todd
Colby

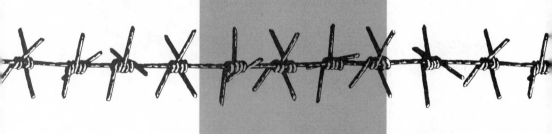

Twenty Songs for My Unborn Fifth Child

I want to teach you how to leap over a fast moving car.
I want to teach you how to get stuck in a window twenty
floors up,
half in, half out.
I want to teach you how to write my name with chalk on the
sidewalk
in front of your house.
I want to teach you how to smack my face when I'm bad.

OH THERE'S SO MUCH TO TEACH YOU!

I want to teach you how to drink a lot of coffee and not
freak out.
I want to teach you how to go to Coney Island all by yourself.
I want to teach you how to dump oatmeal on your
Grandma's bed.
I want to teach you how to load a gun with your teeth.

DO NOT PANIC!

I want to teach you how to get your penis caught
in a vacuum cleaner hose.
Can you turn on a faucet with your ass?
Well today I'm going to show you how.
I want to teach you all about horror and jubilation.
I want to teach you all about panic.

BUT PLEASE, DON'T PANIC YET!

I want to teach you how to tongue kiss a priest
through the confessional screen.
I want to teach you how to joyously slap someone on the back
until their nose begins to bleed.
I want to teach you that a paper towel cylinder is not a sex tool
even if it's full of vaseline.
I want to teach you that a jack ass shall not have a better
car than someone who is really popular.

LOOK AT ME WHEN I'M TEACHING YOU!

I want to teach you all about wonderful holiday rituals.
I want to teach you how to maintain a look of total surprise
as you vomit on your step-mother's lap.
I want to teach you how to stick a dead fish
in the ventilation system of your place of employment.
I want to teach you how to bob for fruit in a bucket of honey.

GET READY TO LEARN!

The Secret

As a teenager I used to secretly put holy water on my zits at Sunday Mass. I thought that by applying the water to the blemishes it would make them heal faster. So, after blessing myself, I would apply what was left of the holy water to my chin or cheek or wherever the zits happened to be. The difficult part was discreetly making the application in the crowded church, yet doing it fast enough so that the water didn't evaporate before reaching the intended target.

Remembering

Even if I remembered climbing trees with you, playing with matches with you, burning plastic army men with you, standing in combat position with you. Stand in the wind like me, the flame like me. Nothing for you but a pine straw sap cap. Nothing in the candy memory of falling down and getting up and riding the bike home with a green apple Now or Later in my mouth. Nothing of the pine tree or the spider's web, welcome home.

The Flue

On monday night a boy was found dead in a chimney. When they opened the flue, his sneakers and jeans dropped onto the grate below. His body was lodged in the chimney. He was drinking heavily, according to a friend. The medics had to break both of his legs in order to pull his body from the flue.

Seize the Pants

the story of our life together
SHORT PANTS

giant-size sofa paintings
WORK PANTS

little neck
DOUBLE KNIT PANTS

roast beef
LATEX PANTS

painful platinum hair
DISCO PANTS

gigantic fucking hair
LEATHER PANTS

surgery
FRUIT PANTS

pistols
HIGH WATER PANTS

quiver pie
SMARTY PANTS

brick cannon trailer
MATERNITY PANTS

the brain needs what it needs
SNOW PANTS

high karate
SWEAT PANTS

the thousand acre smile
TWILL PANTS

tubes
PAINTER'S PANTS

hot water
PANTS, PANTS, PANTS.

Zoom

Everything is frosted and spicy
to The Ecstasy Ritual Dancers.
They made the sky spit meat
while they played checkers with worms.
They photographed a liar
sitting on his bicycle
peeling chrome from the handlebars.
Because they put glue in the brownies
we've been flat on our backs

for over eight hours.
We can't sit with them
because they don't like the way we taste.
Somebody leaned on the fog
and it tipped over
and now they can't see the floor
to fetch a worm
for their checkerboard.
Will they reappear if I wiggle my nose?
Will they make it better?
Will they bring our camera back?
The photo revealed a stool with handlebars
and chrome flakes scattered beneath it.
Don't talk to them,
they don't like the way we taste.
When I dozed off they took a picture
of me sleeping in the bathtub.
Flashes popped over sweater static chimes.
We lived in one room for three days.
The television served as a changing table.
The bath towels were set ablaze for warmth.
We took turns sleeping in the tub.

Cake

I'm so full of cake
If I ate any more cake
I'd have to vomit first
I could eat a cake a day
Sometimes two three cakes
In a single day

I LOVE CAKE

I can't be any clearer than that

I LOVE CAKE

I could eat every cake in New York City
I can't even go into bakeries anymore
Because I'll eat all the cake

I'll say, "Where's the cake?
I love cake
Get me some cake!"

And they'll say,
"We know how much you love cake
And we know that you very rarely
Have the money to buy our cake
So you can't come in here because
You can't afford the cake
But you love cake
So get out of here
You can not have any cake
You don't have the money
To buy any of our cake!"

I'll punch some ass for cake
Gimme all your cake

I WANT CAKE

I WANT YOUR CAKE

GIMME ALL YOUR CAKE

I LOVE CAKE

Get Down!

soothe the penis of the
     drugged poet
         in screeching neon bloomers
        stuff his skinny body
     in a trash compactor
    force him into a tiny booger ball

get down!
  get that disco ball spinning
    slap his cranky flubbings
      add faint S.O.S. distress calls
        to his resume
          and when he's asleep
            stick his finger in a light socket

turn him into a punk
  he's punked out!
    he's heavy
      he's dopey and
        he's grinning—
          he loves this sort of treatment

he's here by your wicked design
  he's waiting for your reptile commands
    he feels so good
      he's ready to die
        kill him!

Matthew
Courtney

A Dream Never Dreamed of Sonny Bono & Don Knotts

Sonny meet Don
Don meet Sonny
I'm thinkin' Sonny Bono
I'm thinkin' Don Knotts
Bono & Knotts
Bono & Knotts
it looks like Bono & Knotts
Bono in Knotts
Bono in my thoughts
Don on all fours
tied up in Knotts
Don Knotts naked in the park
doin' the Sonny Bono
look Ma!
I'm doin' the Bono!
in bed with Sonny
in bed with Bono
gettin' some Bono from Sonny
you get me all tied up in Don Knotts
talkin' Don Knotts
talkin' Don
talkin' that Don Knotts guy
talkin' Knotts
fingers in Knotts
legs in Knotts
neck and head in Knotts
thoughts in Knotts
speech all Bono
poetry
in
Knotts
this aqua-blue Smith-Corona Coronet XL
can hardly record
what Don and Sonny
do with
for
and
to
me.

I'm in It for the Money and the Sex

I'm in it
for the money
and the sex.
I'm in it
for the money
and the sex.
I throw the money around
I throw the sex around
I have the money
I have the sex
I'm in it
for the money
and the sex.
Talkin' about poetry
speakin' about poetry
I'm in it for the money and the sex.
Wads of money
wads of sex
wads! wads! wads!
wads of poetry spit in your face!
Poetry wads comin' at ya!
You'll get your wads worth!
And just like Wadsworth—
I'm in it
for the money
and the sex!

I Wanna Compose Music Damn It!

Have you ever imagined your life as a maestro? I mean
Really and truly?
Some lofty loft or apt apartment would be your paradise.
This dwelling adorned by great green plants and a state of the art
coffee maker from Germany would rule.
Of course, you would have a grand piano, maybe a baby, grand.
or at least an old upright from the Vaudeville days.
A composer would rarely use artificial light—you would have one
or two skylights, or some massive picture windows looking west,
maybe looking east, I don't know . . .
indeed, you'd have a cat.
Named Fluff, or Puss, or Mozart, or Phil.
As a composer, you might smoke. *Yes, I might just smoke.*
But, I mean really smoke. Long thoughtful drags, chin perched on fist,
elbow on piano top, you got your bathrobe and jammies still on,
its like—where do you gotta be?! You just gotta be home!
Windin' out on java, strokin' Fluff and composin',
just plain composin', living a charmed life and making music for
the masses!!
Yeah, youre smoking, like I said, I dunno, Camel Straights, Pall Malls,
Libertines, Havana cigars, maybe some old pipe with some aromatic-
meleiu-makin' tabaccy—
you see, you got these notes in your head, and their spinning and
banging on your cranium, waiting, just waiting to *get down* on paper!
and its great paper too! big sheets of whitish heavy bond,
blank as the day, with these five parallel bars just wafting out
thata way!
And you got this big, scratchy, gold-tipped fountain pen,
just waitin' to wail out these big black notes— *my* hieroglyphs,
in my village that be Greenwich.
And one by one these crazy 'ol notes splash so bold onto the bond,
from the inner recesses of memory, of mystery, of mighty moves and
motion.
Notes caused by the wind in your face, her face, his face, the dog's
face.
This melody from the good, good lovin' that goes good
and the bad, bad lovin' that goes boing!!
Youre livin' a life, a good life, a nice magazine life,
youre a composer

and youre composin' up a storm
or barkin' up a storm (ask Fluff)
youre makin' music for folks to live their lives to,
to come home to, and fold their socks to, to do dinner to, to do the
do to—
and thats a damn good feelin'!!!
People whistling and humming songs that just last year was your hour
in the shower!
Youre complementing and enhancing peoples lives!
Doff your hat to that mirror there baby!

la dee dah sis boom bah tra la la la dee dah fah la lah oh fo sho

that hat (a true story) (my only materialistic poem to date)

I loved that hat
that gray felt Stetson
man I loved it
I wore it
I worked it
I strutted in its shade—
and I lost it.
It felt good to wear that hat
felt complete
felt Stetson
lost my head
when I lost that hat.

Big Stupid Fucker

He's a big stupid fucker
and he's gotta lotta
love to give.

He's a big stupid fucker
and I think he knows it.

Big stupid fucker
you big silly you
big stupid fucker
tickle my toes
tell me your woes.

Big stupid fucker
touch me here
touch me there.

Big stupid fucker
you vacuum
I'll dust
bottom bottom?
Top top?
Dust dust?
Vacuum vacuum?

Big stupid fucker
ya know sumthin' hun—
you're not so big
you're not so stupid
and
you're no fucker neither . . .

Big stupid fucker
I think I love you!
but
I
wanna
know
for
sure!

Big stupid fucker
I think I love you—

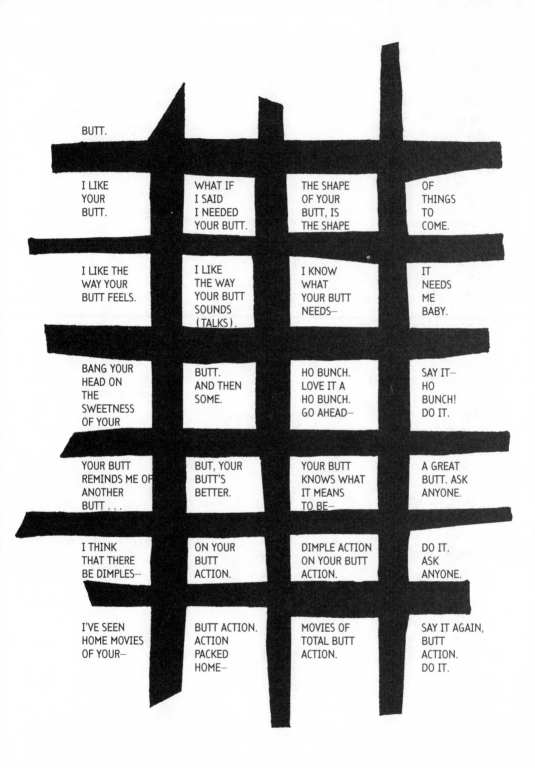

BUTT.

I LIKE
YOUR
BUTT.

WHAT IF
I SAID
I NEEDED
YOUR BUTT.

THE SHAPE
OF YOUR
BUTT, IS
THE SHAPE

OF
THINGS
TO
COME.

I LIKE THE
WAY YOUR
BUTT FEELS.

I LIKE
THE WAY
YOUR BUTT
SOUNDS
(TALKS).

I KNOW
WHAT
YOUR BUTT
NEEDS—

IT
NEEDS
ME
BABY.

BANG YOUR
HEAD ON
THE
SWEETNESS
OF YOUR

BUTT.
AND THEN
SOME.

HO BUNCH.
LOVE IT A
HO BUNCH.
GO AHEAD—

SAY IT—
HO
BUNCH!
DO IT.

YOUR BUTT
REMINDS ME OF
ANOTHER
BUTT . . .

BUT, YOUR
BUTT'S
BETTER.

YOUR BUTT
KNOWS WHAT
IT MEANS
TO BE—

A GREAT
BUTT. ASK
ANYONE.

I THINK
THAT THERE
BE DIMPLES—

ON YOUR
BUTT
ACTION.

DIMPLE ACTION
ON YOUR BUTT
ACTION.

DO IT.
ASK
ANYONE.

I'VE SEEN
HOME MOVIES
OF YOUR—

BUTT ACTION.
ACTION
PACKED
HOME—

MOVIES OF
TOTAL BUTT
ACTION.

SAY IT AGAIN,
BUTT
ACTION.
DO IT.

54

M.
Doughty

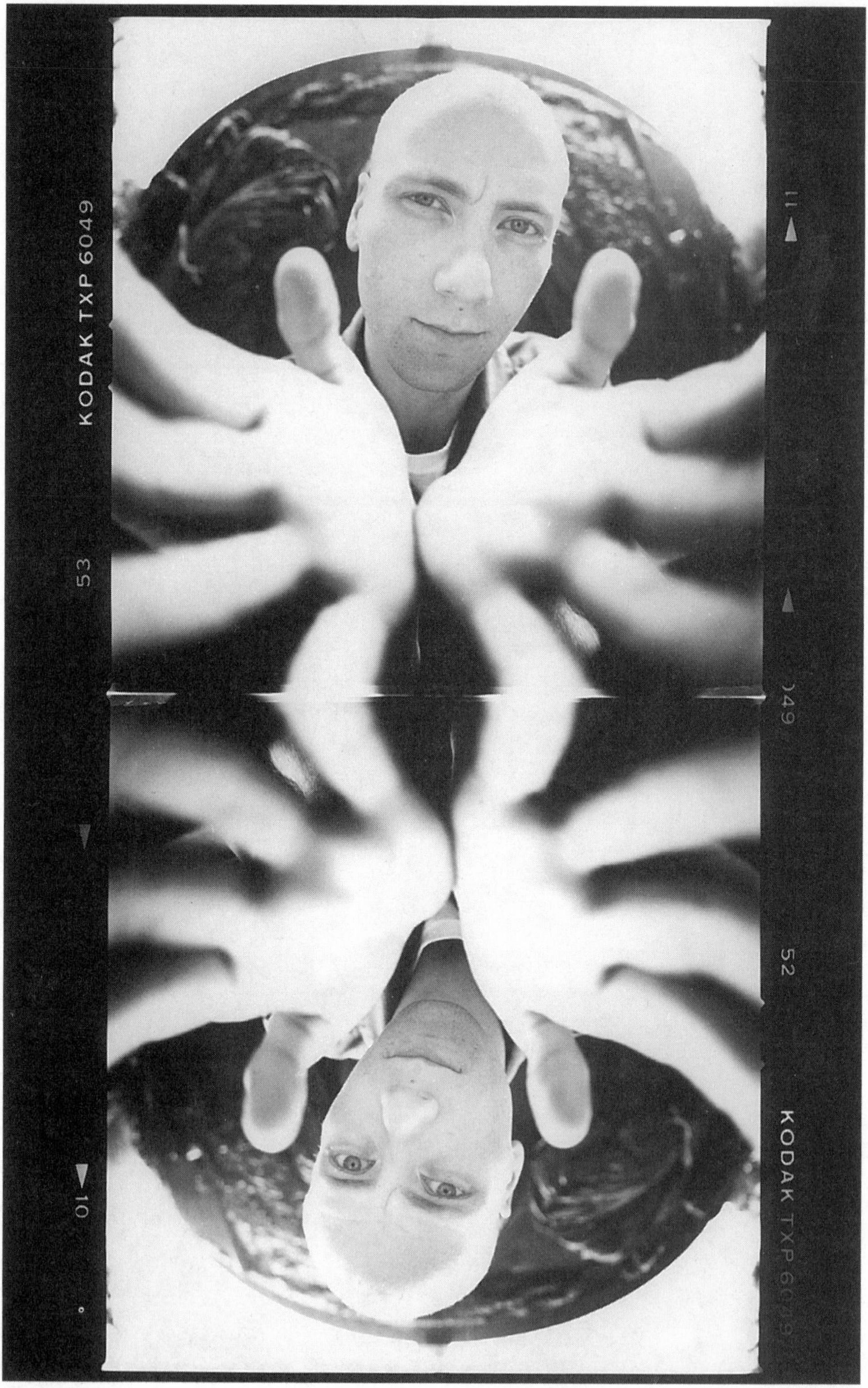
KODAK TXP 6049
53
52

The Bug Wrangler

He was jailed for cruelty to insects, and his agent wasn't answering the phone, so he stayed awake in the cell all night, pictures jumping around his forehead of the cops and blow-dryer they took as evidence. He used the blow-dryer to force the spiders to move, up the arm of a stuntwoman, across a floor. He was known to the industry as a professional, that he could coax wrenching performances from the crankiest bugs. He was a man famed for creating bug performances that would make people weep in the theaters.

They knew what they were jumping into, he thought, I always split the money square, am I wrong? You take some roach out of a miserable life and put it in pictures. Tame the wildest bugs with gloved hands, a flashlight, and a little blow-dryer technology, go to the beasts and teach them respect. Take them into your home and live with them. They betray you to the police for giving them this.

At a press conference, he sat at the microphone with a loyal spider whom he tried to coax a positive character statement out of, but he couldn't use the blow-dryer in front of the media, and the spider stood there and said nothing while he sweated and the videotape rolled on forward.

Nerve Injections

A man has premonitions of his teeth cracking every time he looks at concrete. Like an invisible pain, he can't feel it but his mouth acts as if he can. He feels his teeth as one solid plate, his mouth dammed with china. He becomes so sick of his teeth screaming that he goes to an unlicensed orthodontist in a seedy quarter and is injected in his mouth with painkillers to numb them. He becomes an addict but denies this to himself and walks around pillowed from the world.

Later, he free-falls on ice. He carries his teeth home in his wallet. He reassembles the cracked ones with tile epoxy on his kitchen table. He puts them in the ice tray in his freezer. For the rest of his life a slathering junkie, he gums hard candy unaware that splinters of jawbreaker are slitting gashes in the sockets in his jaw.

Other Fish

A girl with a backpack on a cellular phone sighs;
between the exhale and the first consonant
a van barrels through her. Who knows
what the boy thinks, his line slipping from her voice,
her words sucked backwards through the wire?
Two hours from now he'll be drunk,
his slurred thoughts slobbering over motives,
why she decided suddenly to leave him
and hung up mid-word.

The phone yelps angrily from under a bus,
and she lays splayed like an asterisk
in the dreary sentence of Fourteenth Street.

Cookie Monster as Houdini in a Special Segment

Cookie Monster, burnt out and hateful of children, concocts a suicide ploy under
the auspices of show business; stripped and chained up, he is lifted into a velvet
sack, placed in a steamer trunk full of holes so as to sink faster, sealed, and
thrown into a lake before throngs. The band plays, and in the velvet sack in
the sealed trunk Cookie Monster waits to drown.

Whose Music

He lives in absolute terror of a saxophone he has kept under his bed for four years. He played it since his mouth learned to blow, then put it under the bed four years ago because he had grown bored of it and moved on to affairs with lovelier instruments; a clarinet for two months, a flute for awhile, the drums. He went back to the saxophone and couldn't face it unashamed, so he put it under the bed and learned to play sociology, the jewel of all musical instruments. This all had something to do with the difference between fingerpainting and Jackson Pollock, or Motherwell, or when a man plays stupid noise he finds attractive on a violin he can't play, as opposed to the man who can play études but chooses to screech. The joy, the redemptive power of the horn he felt unentitled to, as if he had to pay more to get his interest back from the saxophone.

Now he fears the saxophone will end up in his mouth like a crack pipe, that twenty years from now he will look back on that one delirious hour with the reed in his mouth, his fingers tapping the brass, and regret it forever. That he will end up some sham Anthony Braxton, always in fear that people will discover him as a fraud. Or that he would spend the rest of his life like Anthony Braxton, scribbling pictures of bicycles and numbers to describe tunes that, language having been stolen from him by the music, he can't name. Yesterday he remembered his affair with the clarinet, momentarily on the D train, over the Manhattan Bridge, and was momentarily swept upward by the memory of the clarinet's wood smell. This somehow coupled with the scenery, the blue riveted-iron bridge that colored his memory like a drink mixed with mathematics and Duke Ellington.

From a Gas Station outside Providence

This kiss, unfinished;
lips to receiver in the parking lot,
a pucker shot through a fiber-optic wire
to an answering machine,
toward switchboards and stations transmitting
in blips to satellites, this kiss
thrown earthward and shooting down
coils, around pipeline and electric power
lumbering underground,
up threads and transistors
and transference points.
This kiss is zeroes and ones jumbled
and tossed into the pneumatic system,
unscrambled at the end and scrawled
onto a tape recorder slowly rolling
at the side of your bed,
then slapping back, reverbed
off the ringer, a tinny phantom
of the smooch like a smack on
an aluminum can, up the same
veins through the belly of the same satellite
and softly to the side of my head;
this kiss is home before the next exhalation leaves.

I'm stooped in the booth,
pounding quarters into the slot;
yellow light droops over the asphalt,
and your ghost, too cool
and elusive with those hands and mouth
sings around me in the smell of gasoline,
Whose mouth is this, scratched in static;
some droplet of a sigh, atomized,
and sputtering digitized into my room?

Kathy
Ebel

Hardcore

You're so hardcore
I can't believe my good fortune
You're so hardcore
Torture me torture me torture me

Your axe in a bag 'cross your back like a shield
Piece in your pocket
Gimme one of them long, smoky looks
and my panties yield
You know you got me ridin' your hand
slidin' in the backseat of a yellow cab
that I had to step to the curb to hail.
We're crossin the Brooklyn Bridge,
my girlhood's set sail
straight to the bottom of the Gowanus Canal &
I can already taste the salty milk of this life lesson

You're so hardcore
Mock the book I'm readin
Punish me for who I am
I'm used to teasin
the kind that hurts
like your fingers, lingerin' over my nipple
across a restaurant table in the middle of the afternoon

Tell me I'm smaller
than the space between your bottom teeth/
I've grown up on disdain
Lecture me stoned on Ancient Egypt and Coltrane
Get real mean if I interrupt you with questions

Please please,
Put words in my pussy
Lie in my bed like a bullet
with your cock
A clenched fist
An angry drill
A slammed door
A snakin' unemployment line

A dream denied
400 years

Leave me in bits and pieces, baby
Arm here
Bitten lip there
Aorta and asshole flung over the back of my desk chair

Fuck me hardcore style
Hands up
Against the wall
Legs apart
I ain't hidin anythin, baby
What you lookin for?

You're so hardcore
You understand the world
You was sellin' Miles eight-balls in Paris
when I was still a scared little girl

You're so hardcore
Let your hate come all over me
I'll drink it
I'm the lover you despise/ who hopes
your rage will yield to sorrow and
you'll let me dry your eyes

This is my contribution
This is my way to earn a place of controversy
on the F train
Mercy
We'll give the yuppies somethin to
nudge nudge wink wink about
maybe somethin to think about
And I'll become the hardcore one
the proud renegade
I'll show off to my girlfriends the turquoise
fingerprint bracelets
you gave me/ all up and down my arms & say

look what my baby made

Sleepover for J.C.

I was always sleeping
when you were
and we were always

sleeping, I was never
awake before you
I was never awake

before this
we
and we were always.

You never slept
with me
watching you sleep,

you slept with me and you next to.

You were never
sleeping when I was
and we were always

this we,
and we always
slept over with this

we of us watching.
You were always awake
and watching over me

sleeping and you next to

sleeping while I watched
over and me next to

and we were always
this we of us

we were sleeping
under and
watching over

Crossing
dedicated to all the yellow traffic lights in new york city

Brave yellow, she blinks
despite chaos passing crazy bold
through holes in the cheesecloth.

In defense of brave yellow, she does
her best to give this action city
an electric breath, some kinda slow.

Brave yellow, she shoos
away a bloody afternoon.

Consider faith as compass
points, bereft of a scarecrow,
teetering on a steeple,

and the citizens, doing their daily dance
along its grid, heads bent to the curb,
praying for points west.

Consider brave yellow. She keeps
the automobiles from the fountains,
hair, tears and rubber

from clogging the gutters, the park
from the airless playground where
the planets rumble,

sharks from jets. And yet, princes
bottomless in grace are stuck to their
rollerskates. They go round

and around the block, battered city maps
memorized, empty passports in
their blue jeans.

Heatwave

And on the ninth day
the Big Asshole gave a snort,
made it real hot like this blister
city's become. The corner
jingle cart's frozen jujus
appeal like a loose fart in
a moldy mailbox. The sad
houseplants won't quit their
whining, they want a weekend
with the Fresh Air Fund,
at least A/C,
a clacking fan,
a stinking drink.

So fuck your new friends in
their pert sundresses. Piss out
the old flame come calling,
all that sweet & eager gone
draggy blanket rancid. Come
on, Steely. Slice the greasy
day. A neat shove with your
cold shoulder's nice.
Being mean beats the heat.
It feels cool.
It feels fine.

Cyberslut

The room is beating. Somebody close the
window, man. I'm floating and crazy.
It feels like goddess to be flying my chair.
The muscles, the muscles are buzzing.

Sweet Jesus, if that man were truly
behind me, as he wrote in the note that
he psuedo and nymmed nice & tight in my
hard drive, and the mouth, and the soft,

the breath, the ear, the oh? We'd slide
inside out. My ass was round & high and
for a while it was shaggy carpet style,
bending over in the private room. Then:

Groans! There's no plug for yearning! No icon
throbbing for The Dive, The Ride, The Grab,
The True Smacking Wrestle Of Me And The Creature!
The beast, my love, cannot be downloaded.

Anne
Elliott

something turned over (for A. Payne)

put his key in monday morning
ignition like always
pumped his foot against the floor, and
waited for the usual sounds

cricket turned a bobbin in his cranium,
maybe, or a memory, like the
crankshaft man that he was, like
the god that he was
my name is Mephistopheles my
*   name is Man-o-War my name*
*   is Man Fucks Whore In A Mor-*
phine bottle my name is Man Fucks More
In A Mine Field my mind is no longer mine, my
mind is no longer whore, you can't buy it anymore
this is fucking payback—
*   back in sixty-nine I did as you pleased, now*
*   I think it's your turn to be me, Money, get*
*   on your goddamn knees*

my name is Mephistopheles my
*   name is Man-o-War my name*
*   is Malaria Mosquito Kicking In Your*
*   Squeaky Clean Screen Door*
I'll draw an American flag in piss
on your welcome mat (welcome home, Al?
well, I'm not Al any more, Uncle,
my name is War) welcome to my world
come on in—pull up an orange agent
orange and I'll tell you a story

once upon a time johnny was dead and johnny was dead and johnny was
*   dead and I don't remember*

THEY TOLD ME TO DRAW YOUR CUNT ON THE WALL LIKE
BABY YOU SAID YOU'D WAIT   THEY TOLD ME TO DRAW
YOUR CUNT ON THE WALL LIKE IT WAS MINE BABY   I'M
JUST FOLLOWING ORDERS   THEY TOLD ME TO STAND
IN YOUR STAIRWELL LIKE A STATUE SOLDIER   I AM IWO JIMA

IN BRONZE I AM CATATONIA IN BRONZE I AM
THE WASHINGTON MONUMENT WASHING
YOUR MOUTH OUT WITH SOAP GIRLFRIEND I'M THE PIN
YOU FORGOT YOU PULLED FROM YOUR HAND GRENADE I'M
THE GOLD BAND YOU FORGOT YOU PULLED FROM YOUR
LEFT HAND I'M THE GOLD FINGER I FORGOT I PULLED FROM THAT
YELLOW ENEMY BODY I'M JUST FRIENDLY   I'M YOUR BEST
SOUVENIR I'M YOUR MEDAL OF HONOR LOVE HONOR AND
OBEY BABY AND I'LL GIVE YOU A BABY I SWEAR
IT WILL SCREAM FROM YOUR CROTCH LIKE CHRISTMAS IT
WILL SWIM THROUGH YOUR FACE LIKE SMILEY TEETH
BREAKFAST TOAST IT WILL NAKED LIKE RUNNING ORPHAN
IT WILL NAPALM LIKE NOBODY'S BUSINESS   BE PREPARED
GIRL SCOUT THIS IS FUCKING PAYBACK

my name is Mephistopheles my
     name is Man-o-War my name
          is Manifest Destiny my name is
               Hitching A Ride To Memphis
my name is Motormouth In Your Ford Taurus my
     name is Money You Owe Me my name
          is Payne In Your Ass, Paine Webber
I'm eating your dollars for breakfast
I'm eating your dollars for breakfast
I'm painting my windshield gold like it's worth it and
I'm melting the keys into coins
I'm melting my car keys into coins
I've got three in my hand right now, see?
This is what it's all about
a penny and
a penny and
a penny

Trojan Love Poems

WON'T YOU PENETRATE THIS WALL
(I BUILT IT JUST FOR THAT PURPOSE)
THERE'S NO HYMEN HERE ANYMORE
(YOU'LL JUST USE THE DOOR)

HE WAS A TRO-JAN
I HANDED HIM A TRO-JAN
JURY SAID IT WAS CONSENT
CAN'T CALL IT RAPE, NOT
RELUCTANT ENOUGH

I WAS A HEL-EN
I HANDED HIM A HELL-O
WON'T YOU COME BACK TO MY PLACE,
HE'LL SAY, I WILL SAY
OKAY

WON'T YOU START A WAR IN MY HONOR
LA LA LA LA LA
WON'T YOU LAUNCH A SHIP IN MY HONOR
LA LA LA LA LA
WON'T YOU WEAR ARMOR IN MY HONOR
LA LA LA LA LA
WON'T YOU MOUNT THIS ANIMAL IN MY HONOR
LA LA LA LA LA
IT'S A BEAUTIFUL DAY ON THE FRONT LINES, I'M
A BEAUTIFUL FRONT IN YOUR FRONT SEAT
WON'T YOU KISS ME GOOD-BYE TONIGHT
WON'T YOU KISS ME HELLO I AM HELEN
I AM HELLO I AM HELL I HATE YOU
LIKE HADES I LOVE YOU LIKE
APHRODITE APPLE TAKE A BITE
IT MIGHT JUST MAKE YOU WANT TO FIGHT

I WAS A HEL-EN
I HANDED HIM A HELL-O
WON'T YOU COME BACK TO MY PLACE,
HE'LL SAY, I WILL SAY,
OKAY

HE WAS A TRO-JAN
I HANDED HIM A TRO-JAN
JURY SAID I WAS CONSENTING
(PARIS SAID I WAS CONFOUNDING)

WRAP YOURSELF IN A STICKY SLEEVE
AND I WILL LET YOU IN
I'LL CLOSE THE GATE BEHIND YOUR HORSE
AND CARNAGE WILL BEGIN, BOY
CLOSE THE GATE BEHIND YOUR HORSE
AND CARNAGE WILL BEGIN.

surf the spittle

the spirit inhabits
the body, like spit.
swap story, or kiss
with other mouths,
a gentle exchange
of humors.

or, evict it. in small globs,
green with bacteria and lost enzymes.

subway platform sign:
NO SPITTING.
I step over fresh puddles
of other selves,
sometimes wade in a
knee-deep spitty city sea.
sometimes a flood, tread water.
angry bile and undertow
promise to suck me under.
I shut my mouth, hold my breath,
a sloppy sidestroke, wait
for seven waves, like sins, to pass.

passive? probably, a man tells me I am.
my energy spent on floating,
exhausted, but humors intact.
wouldn't survive if I were to spit back.

74

Worm Christ

I HEARD TODAY OF A WORM WHO LIVED INSIDE A MAN'S HEAD IT MANEUVERED JUST UNDER HIS SCALP AND COULD NOT BE POISONED OUT THE ONLY WAY THE MAN COULD RID HIMSELF OF THE WORM WAS TO SHAVE HIS HEAD AND STRAP A LARGE STEAK TO HIS CROWN AND DRAWN BY ITS HUNGER THE WORM WOULD BORE ITS WAY THROUGH THE SKIN AND EAT THE HAT OF BEEF

BUT THE WORM WOULD NOT LEAVE WITHOUT LEAVING SOMETHING BEHIND NOTHING COULD BE DONE ABOUT THE WORM'S EXCREMENT BECAUSE SHIT HAS NO DESIRE DOES NOT REQUIRE NOURISHMENT

AND THE MAN'S HAIR WOULD SPROUT BACK FERTILIZED BY WORM DROPPINGS

AND THE WORM'S SHIT WOULD SLOWLY DISINTEGRATE BUT WOULD NEVER LEAVE THE MAN'S BODY AND WE WOULD EVENTUALLY FIND ITS TRACES IN HIS BLOOD

I HEARD TODAY OF A THING CALLED CHRIST WHO LIVED INSIDE A WOMAN'S HEAD IT MANEUVERED JUST UNDER HER SCALP AND COULD NOT BE POISONED OUT THE ONLY WAY THE WOMAN COULD RID HERSELF OF THE CHRIST WAS TO SHAVE HER HEAD AND STRAP A LARGE QUESTION TO HER CROWN AND DRAWN BY ITS HUNGER THE CHRIST WOULD BORE ITS WAY THROUGH THE SKIN AND TRY TO ANSWER THE QUESTION

BUT THE CHRIST WOULD NOT LEAVE WITHOUT LEAVING SOMETHING BEHIND NOTHING COULD BE DONE ABOUT THE CHRIST'S WORDS BECAUSE WORDS SPOKEN LONG AGO HAVE NO DESIRE DO NOT REQUIRE NOURISHMENT AND THE WOMAN'S HAIR WOULD SPROUT BACK FERTILIZED BY OLD WORDS

AND THE CHRIST'S OLD WORDS WOULD SLOWLY DISINTEGRATE BUT WOULD NEVER LEAVE THE WOMAN'S BODY AND WE WOULD EVENTUALLY FIND TRACES IN HER BLOOD

Janice
Erlbaum

Sonnet 25

I lost 2 men somewhere, at least
I thought they'd been there, mixed up
with my age I guess I don't know anymore
who I fucked before, or when it counts

I made a list of names, it came up short
the last few years were easy, thinking
steady lovers staggered by *how old were you*
14, that's one for every

year I've been around, but now I'm off,
where 25 was round and safely ended, I was
bluntly intercepted by the present, 25

a book I wrote and closed, I opened
diaries and couldn't find the missing lovers—
as the past gets old the numbers shrink

fellas sestina

across the street from washington square, a stoop
littered with burst butts, torn leaves, dead
bugs, things we could kill or rip apart, girls
waiting, pretending not to wait, drinking beers
pinkies and eyebrows raised, waiting for us—
for us, it was a summer of much fucking

back when boys were angry kings of fucking,
fighting, getting drunk, the order of the stoop
set in brownstone between us, sworn among us
night and night again, saluted in the dead
of drunk summer, christened to soaking with beers,
wrestled into bare hugs, *homos,* scoffed the girls

there was the fellas and then there was the girls
the fellettes, or fellatios, if they were fucking
and they were always fucking, after a couple beers
there was the girls, defaulting at our feet on the stoop
all other august possibilities exhausted or dead
the girls fell tough, always trying to outdrink us

in dead-end games, the solace of stupor, relief to us
thin and whistling, the high sound of girls
singing the summer radio like ether, like ron was dead
coming back from the beach leaned out the fucking
C train window, *look ma, no head,* stupid
accident, boys being boys, too much lsd and beers

squinting at the dregs of our pints and beers
something hurtling early towards death made us
crave breaking glass, splinter empties against the stoop
saw us break each other's noses over girls
we all closed our eyes while fucking
got fucked up, and graduated into the dead

together endured the friendship of the dead
wait of summer after high school, passing beers
and time, like the stupid music of dumb fucking,
slowed to a tocking throb, a pounding around us
dull late into the night, our arms around the girls
we sat stock-still against the earths turning, did not fall
          forward off the stoop

oh fuck bring me back now to the stoop of the dead
altar of boys, where the girls were brilliant sluts drinking sweet beers
toasting us, and waiting to get on with the fucking

Your Psychic Friend (excerpt)

You are a thirty-two-year-old woman who drinks too much and calls herself baby in private. I envision you on the floor of your bathroom, rocking, arms locked around your knees, crying *baby*. Sauced, thinking about carbon monoxide and pills. Still blaming yourself for the miscarriage, I see.

"It was an abortion," you tell me.

"I'm glad you called," I say.

You are a fifty-six-year-old man who wants to know about numbers. I want to tell you that no number is lucky, because no number exists. Numbers are ideas, they only matter if you attach them to facts. You owe some person thirty-five thousand individual facts of U.S. currency, which is worth more to this person than the idea of your entire life.

"What are my numbers," you want to know. I think of you in your temporary home, your ashes and zeros.

"Thirty-six," I say. "Twenty-two. Forty-five." Nothing.

You are a twenty-three-year-old manicurist who lives with her mother and her two babies in the Bronx. You love the soap opera starring the actor who appears on our commercials, first he was a rapist, but now he's good. There is one man in your life who is older who is in love with you. Then there is your boyfriend who sets small fires. "I can't really afford to call like this but there's a lot I need to know."

"Yes, I see," I say, predictably, your credit report up on my screen. "In the not too distant future, your Visa will be cut off."

This is the only way I can help you. I can't lift things with my eyes or read symbols through cards, I don't bend spoons or talk to the dead. But I can think about you. I think about you all the time, conjure you between calls. I pass you on the street and remember you later, think of you filling out the rest of your life like a survey: job, hobby, source of greatest shame. I never forget a face. I could pick you from a crowd. I want you to know, I want everyone to know, I am thinking of you.

Love Letter to His Dick

Dear His Dick,

   You, I miss! And now that he's out of the picture, I think I can finally admit—it was you I loved all along! Yes of course, my darling, you! You never told me I was crazy! You thought my hair looked fine! Our communication was perfect, why, we always knew just what the other wanted, and you always took my side, don't think I didn't notice! Oh, I saw how mutely you loved me, how you rose to meet my sotto murmur—oh, for those moments we stole alone! Away from the mouth, that fickle asshole, when I held you to my breast and we*—we were so happy together**—why did it have to end?*** Life without you is empty! I miss you! Why don't you leave him, and come away with me? Yes, my darling, we'll elope! This is how I imagine you—hopping bravely across the street on your balls to see me! You always should have been mine, I knew what to do with you better than he did! He abused you as much as he did me! Well, we'll show him, won't we darling? He can't keep us apart!

*(sobs)
**(sobs sobs)
***(sobs sobs sobs)

Old Me

Hello, it's me—yes, you, us
again, it's me again, hello,
old me, same me from mirrors
and other optical phenomena,
so here we are again, having
conversations alone, like we
were sixteen and tripping on acid
in a deli! And there we were,
do you remember? And we were
rapturous to see me, as we'd
often hoped and suspected me
there, and we touched the finger
to the mirror with overjoy and
understanding, knowing *nobody
knows what we know and I'm
glad we're together now, let's
say how things really are for us.
I love you. I miss you all the time.
I'm sorry things are so tough.
Oh god I'll see you later.* And
so I was my halo, my body's subtle
self, and went bereft for weeks
without me, then feeling me step
suddenly into my absence like

an ocean entering a room, a bird
landing in its own shadow and
taking flight, until I learned to live
without you. So now I'm not you
anymore, I'm me, though it's still
us, it'll always be us, and I do feel
fondly, even with the disasters,
    tender
every time we emanate together
    and
wonder, I've thought you were a
chimera, or a penumbra, or a
    word
you're not sure what it means but
you use anyway, and which one is
    me,
and if you are apocryphal like the
fiction, I wonder why you disavow
me, and who it is I think I see
    standing
two feet deep in the mirror
    tonight.
Hello. Who is this again. I'm me.
It's us, and it's been so long.

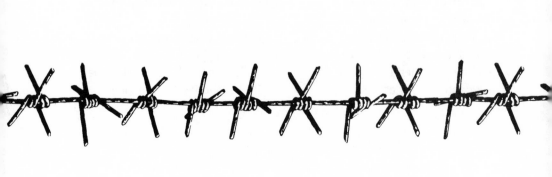

Allen
Ginsberg

I Am a Victim of Telephone

When I lie down to sleep dream the Wishing Well it rings
"Have you a new play for the brokendown theater?"
When I write in my notebook poem it rings
"Buster Keaton is under the brooklyn bridge on Frankfurt and Pearl . . ."
When I unsheath my skin extend my cock toward someone's thighs fat or
    thin, boy or girl
Tingaling—"Please get him out of jail . . . the police are crashing down"
When I lift the soupspoon to my lips, the phone on the floor begins
    purring
"Hello it's me—I'm in the park two broads from Iowa . . . nowhere to sleep
    last night . . . hit 'em in the mouth"
When I muse at smoke crawling over the roof outside my street window
purifying Eternity with my eye observation of gray vaporous columns in
    the sky
ring ring "Hello this is Esquire be a dear and finish your political
    commitment manifesto"
When I listen to radio presidents roaring on the convention floor
the phone also chimes in "Rush up to Harlem with us and see the riots"
Always the telephone linked to all the hearts of the world beating at once
crying my husband's gone my boyfriend's busted forever my poetry was
    rejected
won't you come over for money and please won't you write me a piece of
    bullshit
How are you dear can you come to Easthampton we're all here bathing in
    the ocean we're all so lonely
and I lie back on my pallet contemplating $50 phone bill, broke, drowsy,
    anxious, my heart fearful of the fingers dialing, the deaths, the
    singing of telephone bells
ringing at dawn ringing all afternoon ringing up midnight ringing now
    forever.

Please Master

Please master can I touch your cheek
please master can I kneel at your feet
please master can I loosen your blue pants
please master can I gaze at your golden haired belly
please master can I gently take down your shorts
please master can I have your thighs bare to my eyes
please master can I take off my clothes below your chair
please master can I kiss your ankles and soul
please master can I touch lips to your hard muscle hairless thigh
please master can I lay my ear pressed to your stomach
please master can I wrap my arms around your white ass
please master can I lick your groin curled with blond soft fur
please master can I touch my tongue to your rosy asshole
please master may I pass my face to your balls,
please master, please look into my eyes,
please master order me down on the floor,
please master tell me to lick your thick shaft
please master put your rough hands on my bald hairy skull
please master press my mouth to your prick-heart
please master press my face into your belly, pull me slowly strong thumbed
till your dumb hardness fills my throat to the base
till I swallow & taste your delicate flesh-hot prick barrel veined Please
Master push my shoulders away and stare in my eye, & make me bend over
    the table
please master grab my thighs and lift my ass to your waist
please master your hand's rough stroke on my neck your palm down my
    backside
please master push me up, my feet on chairs, till my hole feels the breath of
    your spit and your thumb stroke
please master make me say Please Master Fuck me now Please
Master grease my balls and hairmouth with sweet vaselines
please master stroke your shaft with white creams
please master touch your cock head to my wrinkled self-hole
please master push it in gently, your elbows enwrapped round my breast
your arms passing down to my belly, my penis you touch w / your fingers
please master shove it in me a little, a little, a little,
please master sink your droor thing down my behind
& please master make me wiggle my rear to eat up the prick trunk
till my asshalfs cuddle your thighs, my back bent over,

till I'm alone sticking out, your sword stuck throbbing in me
please master pull out and slowly roll into the bottom
please master lunge it again, and withdraw to the tip
please please master fuck me again with your self, please fuck me Please
Master drive down till it hurts me the softness the
Softness please master make love to my ass, give body to center, & fuck me
      for good like a girl,
tenderly clasp me please master I take me to thee,
& drive in my belly your selfsame sweet heat-rood
you fingered in solitude Denver or Brooklyn or fucked in a maiden in Paris
      carlots
please master drive me thy vehicle, body of love dops, sweat fuck
body of tenderness, Give me your dog fuck faster
please master make me go moan on the table
Go moan O please master do fuck me like that
in your rhythm thrill-plunge & pull-back-bounce & push down
till I loosen my asshole a dog on the table yelping with terror delight to be
      loved
Please master call me a dog, an ass beast, a wet asshole,
& fuck me more violent, my eyes hid with your palms round my skull
& plunge down in a brutal hard lash thru soft drip-fish
& throb thru five seconds to spurt out your semen heat
over & over, bamming it in while I cry out your name I do love you
please Master.

Punk Rock Your My Big Crybaby

I'll tell my deaf mother on you! Fall on the floor
and eat your grandmother's diapers! Drums,
Whatta lotta Noise you want a Revolution?
Wanna Apocalypse? Blow up in Dynamite Sound?
I can't get excited, Louder! Viciouser!
Fuck me in the ass! Suck me! Come in my ears!
I want those pink Abdominal bellybuttons!
Promise you'll murder me in the gutter with Orgasms!
I'll buy a ticket to your nightclub, I wanna get busted!
50 years old I wanna Go! with whips & chains & leather!
Spank me! Kiss me in the eye! Suck me all over
from Mabuhay Gardens to CBGB's coast to coast
Skull to toe Gimme yr electric guitar naked,
Punk President, eat up the FBI w/ yr big mouth.

Old Pond

The old pond—a frog jumps in, kerplunk!
Hard road! I walked till both feet stunk—
Ma!Ma! Whatcha doing down on that bed?
Pa!Pa! what hole you hide your head?

Left home got work down town today
Sold coke, got busted looking gay
Day dream, I acted like a clunk
Th'old pond—a frog jumps in, kerplunk!

Got hitched, I bought a frying pan
Fried eggs, my wife eats like a man
Won't cook, her oatmeal tastes like funk
Th'old pond—a frog jumps in, kerplunk!

Eat shit exactly what she said
Drink wine, it goes right down my head
Fucked up, they all yelled I was drunk
Th'old pond—a frog jumps in, kerplunk!

Saw God at six o'clock tonight
Flop house, I think I'll start a fight
Head ache like both my eyeballs shrunk
Th'old pond—a frog jumps in, kerplunk!

Hot dog! I love my mustard hot
Hey Rube! I think I just got shot
Drop dead She said you want some junk?
Th'old pond—a frog jumps in, kerplunk!

Oh ho your dirty needle stinks
No no I don't shoot up with finks
Speed greed I stood there with the punk
Th'old pond—a frog jumps in, kerplunk!

Yeh yeh gimme a breath of fresh air
Guess who I am well you don't care
No name call up the mocking Monk
Th'old pond—a frog jumps in, kerplunk!

No echo, make a lot of noise
Come home you owe it to the boys
Can't hear you scream your fish's sunk
Th'old pond—a frog jumps in, kerplunk!

Just folks, we bought a motor car
No gas I guess we crossed the bar
I swear we started for Podunk
Th'old pond—a frog jumps in, kerplunk!

I got his banjo on my knee
I played it like an old Sweetie
I sang plunk-a-plunk-a-plunk plunk plunk plunk
Th'old pond—a frog jumps in, kerplunk!

One hand I gave myself the clap
Unborn, but still I took the rap
Big deal, I fell out of my bunk
Th'old pond—a frog jumps in, kerplunk!

Hey hey! I ride down the blue sky
Sit down with worms until I die
Fare well! Hū . m Hū . m Hū . m Hū . m Hū . m Hū . m!
Th'old pond—a frog jumps in, kerplunk!

Red barn rise wet in morning dew
Cockadoo dle do oink oink moo moo
Buzz buzz—flyswatter in the kitchen, thwunk!
Th'old pond—a frog jumps in, kerplunk!

John
Giorno

Pornographic Poem (1965)

Seven Cuban
army officers
in exile
were at me
all night.
Tall,
sleek,
slender,
Hispanic types
with smooth dark
muscular bodies
and hair
like wet coal
on their heads
and between their legs.
I lost count
of the times
I was fucked
by them
in every conceivable
position.
At one point
they stood
around me
in a circle
and I had
to crawl
from one crotch
to another
sucking
on each cock
until it was hard.
When I got all
seven up,
I shivered
looking up
at those erect pricks,
all different lengths
and widths,
and knowing
that each one

was going up
my ass hole.

Everyone
came
at least twice
and some three times.
Once they put me
on the bed
kneeling,
one fucked me
in the behind,
another face fucked
my mouth,
while I jacked off
one
with each hand,
and two others
rubbed
their dicks
on my bare feet
waiting
their turns
to get
in my butt.
Just when I thought
they were all spent,
two of them
got together,
and fucked me
at once
The positions
we were in
were crazy,
but with two
big fat
Cuban cocks
up my ass
at one time,
I was
in paradise.

95

Just Say
No
to Family Values

On a day when
you're walking down the street
and you see a hearse
with a coffin,
followed by a flower car
and limos,
you know the day
is auspicious,
your plans are going to be
successful,
but on a day when
you see a bride and groom,
and a wedding party,
be careful,
watch out,
it might be a bad sign.

Just say no
to family values,
and don't quit
your day job.

Drugs
are sacred
substances,
and some drugs
are very sacred
substances,
too much
is not enough,
please praise them
for somewhat liberating
the mind.

Tobacco
is a sacred substance
to some,

96

and even though you've stopped
smoking,
show a little respect.

Alcohol
is totally great,
let us celebrate
the glorious qualities
of booze,
and I had
a good
time
with you.

Just
do it,
just don't
not do it,
just do it.

Christian
fundamentalists,
and fundamentalists in general,
are viruses,
and they're destroying us,
multiplying
and mutating,
they're killing us,
now, you know,
you gotta give
strong medicine
to combat
a virus.

Who's buying,
good acid,
I'm flying,
slipping
and sliding,
slurping
and slamming,
I'm sinking,
dipping
and dripping,

and squirting inside you;
never fast forward
a cum shot;
milk, milk,
lemonade,
go around
the corner where
the chocolate's made;
I love to see
your face
when you're
suffering.

Do it
with anybody
you want,
whatever
you want,
for as long as you want,
anytime,
any place,
when it's possible,
and try
to be safe;
in a situation where
you must completely
abandon yourself
beyond all concepts.

Twat throat
and cigarette dew,
that floor would ruin
a sponge mop,
she's the queen of great bliss,
and in your heart
is a lightbulb
radiating
great clarity,
in your heart,
and flowing up
in a crystal channel
into your eyes,
and out
hooking

the world
with compassion.

Just say
No
to family
values
just say No to family values.

We don't have to say No
to family values,
cause we never think
about them.
Just
do it,
just make love
and compassion.

(1995)

John
S. Hall

To Walk Among the Pigs

To walk among the pigs
To go where the pigs go and do as the pigs do
To inhale the pungent stench of the pigs and truly savor the scent
To sing the song of the pigs
To build up a rapport, to be one with the pigs
To work shoulder to shoulder with the pigs on pig-like projects
To sweat like a pig and then to realize that pigs never sweat

To wallow in the mud with the pigs
To experience absolutely all that pigness entails
To hear. To see. To feel like a pig
To think, eat and smell like a pig
To comprehend completely what it is to be a pig
To fully understand that you and the pigs and all other things in the universe
     are of
the same ilk
And then . . .
To weed out all non-pig things, to fully cultivate and allow to blossom the
     flower that is the pig within your soul
And to finally stand alone, in the garden of the Absolute and pray and prey
     and pray like a pig

Let's Have Sex

I will slur
And heel and hem and haw
I will eat a monkey paw
When you call me up and command me to come over to your house for sex
     and tea
biscuits, I shall clandestinely drop my cummerbund down the dumbwaiter
     chute.
Lutes will serenade us like liquid lemonade.
You will glisten like newborn snow, and I will listen like a clairvoyant nipple
     clamp.

It will be sex, like nobody has ever had it before in the history of
    postmodern lovemaking.
It will be sex, even if it isn't.
It will be sex, even if only in theory, even if it's only pantomime,
even if it's just a memory, or a dream or a symphonic approximation;
after a summer of autonomous sodomy and national geographic specials
    about pretty
animals that use other little animals as food, by eating them,
on television.
But we shouldn't even watch television, we should just have sex:
epoch making, earth shaking,
teeth chattering, dish clattering,
fish frying, eye popping,
never stopping, bunny hopping,
toe tapping, Joseph Papping sex.
Shakespeare in the park kinda sex.
D train ride to Coney Island vacation kinda sex.
Clandestine in the airplane lavatory kind of sex.

Olympic marathon sex,
All the different ways that we feel like having sex, we should,
until we grow old and bored and disillusioned.
Then let us rekindle our feelings,
forget our despair and our celibate nonsense
and fuck like bunnyrats till the cows come home to roost.
So call me sometime, and let's have sex.

It's Saturday

I want to be different, like everybody else I want to be like
I want to be just like all the different people
I have no further interest in being the same, because I have seen difference
    all around,
and now I know that that's what I want

I don't want to blend in and be indistinguishable,
I want to be a part of the different crowd,
and assert my individuality along with others
who are different like me

I don't want to be identical to anyone or anything
I don't even want to be identical to myself

I want to look in the mirror and wonder,
"Who is that person? I've never seen that person before.
I've never seen anyone like that before."
I want to call into question the very idea that identity can be attached
I want a floating, shifting, ever-changing persona
Invisibility and obscurity,
detachment from the ego and all of its pursuits.
Unity is useless
Conformity is competitive and divisive and leads only to stagnation and
    death.

If what I'm saying doesn't make any sense,
that's because sense can not be made
It's something that must be sensed
And I, for one, am incensed by all of this complacency
Why oppose war only when there's a war?
Why defend the clinics only when they're attacked?
Why support the squats and the parks only when the police come to close
    them down?
Why are we always reactive?
Let's activate something
Let's fuck shit up
Whatever happened to revolution for the hell of it?
Whatever happened to protesting nothing in particular, just protesting 'cause
    it's
Saturday and there's nothing else to do?

The Evil Children

And so
The very evil children
Took the dog out to play in the park

Then they took him home
And refused
To set him on fire

They were evil, evil, evil children
And they refused to do
As they were told

They would say,
"Why should we leave the elderly woman
In the middle of the Expressway?
Fuck you, we're not doing it."

Then they would go downstairs
And prepare
The Molotov cocktails.

Knowing full well
That when they were finished,

There was no way in hell
They were gonna blow up
The neighbors' barn
They were evil, evil, evil children.

All their lives,
People expected them to do bad.
They almost
Never delivered[1]

How Much Longer?

I want the car to explode when you drive me to the K-mart.
I want you to solder my face to the mighty oak tree.
I want to fuck myself with my atom bomb.
Why is it that I cannot, not even only once, find glass in my dinner or razor
        blades in
the bedsheets?
I pay my taxes.
When will my hard work and dedication pay off?
When will I reap what I have sown?
When will my tiny penis shrivel up and disappear?

[1]Last verse stolen from Roger Manning.

When will my testicles bleed with joy?
When will I drown in urine and vomit and my menstrual juices?
I want to be the lamb slaughtered in the Milk Bar.
I want to live.
I want to live.
I want to die.
I want to live.
How much longer must I wait?

I'm Sorry

No, I never was in Vietnam
I never once dove into an empty swimming pool
I never let the carpet walk right out from under me
I never painted a house or a tree
I never did become an exotic dancer, or a customer service representative
I never took the pulse of a dying duck, or gave mouth-to-mouth resuscitation
    to a horsefly
In a way, I suppose you could say that my experience is quite limited
For example, I never locked Oliver Cromwell in a broom closet while singing
    Waltzing
Matilda
I never sawed a television in half, although I once saw Wendy O. Williams
    saw a guitar
I never played a decent game of jacks
I never played poker with a toothless one-eyed pirate who kept picking his
    teeth with a
bowie knife to distract me, while his parrot looked over my shoulder and
    told him what
cards I had by using an elaborate code involving vomiting, chirping, and sea
    chanteys
I never bought a lamp—wait—I did buy a lamp once
But I never bought a lantern, or a lambskin prophylactic
I never bought lima beans or lime pudding
I never bought a lion or a Lionel Richie album
I never bought anything beginning with the letter "L" except lollipops, light
    bulbs and
lettuce and the lamp
I never laid down for a nap and found the Everly Brothers in bed with me
I never let a cyborg take out the garbage

I'm sorry
I stole the radio
I did it
I sawed the legs off the periodic table
I re-elected the president
I did it, it was my fault
I farted in the church
I'm sorry
I did many many bad things and I am so sorry

Bob
Holman

The Has—Been Poet to Gaston Neal

The has-been poet is back
The over-the-hill poet suddenly is not only not over it
But king of it queen of it prince and princess kiss the frog
Royalty of it be damned of it shouting lungsful from far atop
Mount Poem where you never been hell you never seen
It so shrouded in the cloudy foggy do-do
Of your own shortsighted need contacts to look in the mirror
Steam face clearing and what do you finally see see see
Samo samo samo samo
That's you-o
Somewhere in there-o
Holding on to the scraps of your control panel
Attached to goddamn
Ain't attached whahappen whahappen

While the usta be poet, why
The usta be poet never went away
And all your workshops and accreditation programs
All your grants and fundraising gala soirees wait till it's served
Before you touch it goddamn don't drink it all in the first half-hour
All the be home in time to let the sitter go home
But where is home?
Now you see it's not that I'm anti-family
I am pro-family
I just think you better redefine what constitutes your own goddamn
        family
Cause when you say whatever crossed the transom goes before the
        committee
I say guess who's coming to dinner? Why, it's the has-been poet
And guess what? he's staying over for breakfast too
And guess what else she's making you your lunch as well because
Guess what, she's a transgender transgenerational mixed-race
        motherfucker of a has-been poet
And I'm back cause guess what
I never went away
Where you been, fool?

No Dream

Went down to the shop
Like every morning—wearing
My red suit—strange
Old woman came in—all
I remember. Next a family,
I'm the papa, I don't
Recognize them. They're
Breaking down our door
I wrote the wrong door
The angels won't let us use
The ladders I climb anyway
The moon translates—See me
Pinned down there with love
And dependence. Thus I
Sleep at last with my own
Family, all dressed in red.
Demons guard our feet,
Angels our head.

Poem for My Daughters in the New Year

Diving straight down at our red chimney
The green is powering up at me

Electric lines are giving off blue sparks
The clouds are layers of white and pink sharks

I see the City like Oz over my wing
What can I give you now, anything?

Sophie, you are twelve and making up a world brashly
Daisy, you are nine and dreaming in an envelope cozily

I have a poem for each of you, with love and your name
Because to me they mean the same

A Jew in New York

Like everybody else, I wasn't a Jew
Until I came to New York. In Portland, OR,
The other day, a young Latina asked me
If I were Jewyorican. Papa and Bubby
Came from Ukraine, landed in Brooklyn,
Settled in Harlan, KY, and named my father
Benjamin Franklin. My mother, the offspring
Of a coal miner, married Ben, the only Jew
In town. He didn't last. Ma remarried.
In kindergarten, in Cincinnati, instead
Of moving to the Afternoon session the second

Semester, I stayed in Morning and changed my name.
This is the year 5755. In Chinese it is Year
Of the Dog. I am 45 years old and learn that
The days between Rosh Hashanah and Yom Kippur
Are the Days of Awe. Moody and gray, with dashes
Of absolute clarity, I love this season. Cleansing
The summer's sweat from the streets of New York,
I always think of the Year beginning in September.
"That's when school starts." A holdover from youth.
This year, 1994, for the first time I thought,
Hey, it's the real New Year, and I am a real Jew.
A real Jew and a real coal miner's son, too.

Later for Now

Bird whistles worms dance
I am your little survivor, Baby.
The delicate penumbra of you
And your family's belief system
Rocks me like the sea, deep
And deadly. Who needs narcotics
When I can make up with you
Or wake up and see you and wake you
Beside me. Wake up wake up
The emergency bellows of heaven
Are crying for a quick Apocalypse
Over your dead body. I will wake you
Because the Jews 30 A.D. wrapped the dying
And when he said the magic poem, up rose
Ol Lazarus like the so-called brain-dead
For a last slab of ecstasy.

Plunking on the banjo with you
On my knee. Digging up the jar
We planted in Tennessee.

Principal Reason

I am in love with you
I want to rub feet in bed
Please invent beds

Because of You

Everything is you
Especially our children
Please pay the rent

Good Morning

Eating breakfast words
Family cereal box
Conversation flakes

Prison

More drugs in than out
Licking sex, tossing salad
So much to learn here!

Parking Meter

I am a happy
Parking meter tickticktick
Feed me, Muthfukka

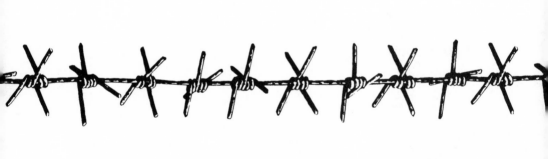

Christian X.
Hunter

Poemfone Fever

I'll bet you think it's easy making up a new poem every morning for you all. Just coffee and donuts and sittin' round the telephone. Well it's not! It's torture in the tar pits. Weather's triggering flood after flood of memory; my heart's been pounding since I woke up—a bad case of thermonuclear jump-the-gun spring fever; the kind that may lead to colossal, abstruse melancholy or unrestrained joy. I'm awash with the overwhelming sense of imminent possibilities for great promise or for deep bottomless pits of failure. Too many possibilities, like anxiety angels waiting coyly, arms crossed, in doorways on played-out boulevards where the dead-headed meaningless sun will soon arrive, possibility—like being a virgin in summer, possibility—like waking up in a strange bed, like afternoon thunderheads rolling in at the beach, like goosebumps on a bride's arm, like icy sweat on a patrolman's neck, possibilities—running wild like a herd of swine in the canyons of Soho on a Sunday. My head is throbbing. I got a life flashing before my eyes and it ain't even mine—I think maybe it's Willie Loman's or Bob Holman's! It's wearing me out. Whew!!! It's like being in love only I don't know what you look like way out there at the end of this here telephone line. Still I'm thinking; ain't this a lush trip. It makes me wonder how many dream-chained poets are quietly going mad in their tiny East Village studios on this frozen morning.

For
Buddy

Stop working
the lobster
shift at the
paper bag
factory, Sleep
late get rich
fuck what
your friends
say, Drive an
Artaud-
mobile with a
Boyz in the
Hood
ornament—
keep the
drunks in the
trunk, Fade
Lucky Seven
in the rear-
view mirror,
Navigate
head to toe
covered in
chorus girls,
Stop to steal
flowers from
the
millionaire
cemetery give
'em to yer ma
on the day
after Mother's
Day, Lock up
the kids in
the basement
of Bellevue,
Pass on every
waitress with
bitch
mannerisms,
Pick up the
tab for that
juke-box last
gleaming &
dance again
dance again
dance your
way down
stream
Show up in
Heaven
wearing silk
pajamas.

Off the Air

The Woman Who Sleeps
While the Window Fan Hums
The Falling Down Drunk
In the Apartment Above
The Cigarette Burns
On the Blue Pillow Case
The Sound of a Toilet
Being Flushed in the Hall
Faint Cigarette Smoke
Drifts Up From the Street
Cats . . . Enter and Leave
Through the Fire Escape Window
Cotton and Matches
On a Small Kitchen Table
The Soothing Smell
Of Sweet Cooling Roof Tar
The Phone Disconnected
Forever and Ever
Her Two Perfect Hands
The Palms Pressed Together
She's my Prayer in the Stillness
She is the Absence of Angels
I Kiss the Small of Her Back
And Lie Down Beside Her
In the Endless Moondrift
Of Her No Dream Surrender
And the Vampire Rapture
Of Radio Silence.

Deuce Poem

I've always loved Manhattan in the hot weather. As a small kid I would be sent away to stupid summer camps in the country. I hated them. While being forced to learn the breast stroke in ice-cold water in some mountain lake, I'd be wishing I was at the heavily chlorinated Twenty-third Street pool near the East River, surrounded by thousands of New Yorkers playing and shouting in dozens of languages. While sitting around the campfire with my eyes tearing from smoke and burning my mouth trying to suck some shitty marshmallow off a pointed stick, I'd be thinking about how I'd rather be on Manhattan Avenue hanging out on the hood of a car, downing a slice with Paul, Eddy or Hector.

There was never a moment when I wasn't missing the gritty yellow brightness of Times Square at night, switchblades and sex toys, inflatable Oh!-mouthed latex love dolls—shelves lined with pimp hats, the glaring green fluorescence of the Playland arcades on Seventh Avenue, their windows full of clown masks, fake I.D.s and pissing statues, or the late-night fast-food snack cemeteries, where artistically basted month-old chickens turn over in perpetuity in glass and metal coffins alongside dusty tombstone Bisquick boxes, desiccated cereals, Tampax and miniature bottles of Pepto-Bismol. Yeah, you know, there wasn't a minute spent in those green, pine-scented fields when I wasn't missing the dull surprise of being caught by head-on blasts of hot greasy air from the kitchen exhausts of Mi Chinita and La Taza D'Oro, the vivid sanctity of bleeding Jesus botanicas, or the morbid and unnatural colors of internal-organ-shaped mutant foodstuffs piled up in the glass cases of the *cuchifrito* stands on Ninth Avenue. Fields of daisies pale beside the flash-and-spin birds of paradise cruising up Christopher Street, the restless shadow cowboys by the West Side Highway, and the chain-mail leather dogs at the hot fudge sex show. Hiking in wheat fields and serene walks down paths alongside clear running brooks don't signify next to the freedom to walk from Fourth Street to Fourteenth Street to Forty-second Street, not needing a passport, the way mist touches the back of your neck as you cross the street to avoid an open fire hydrant, or Heinekens and *pasteles* with hot sauce eaten barefoot out on the end of the pier at Coney Island. Looking down from atop some lofty peak in the White Mountains will never produce the little shudder of mute and detached white boy's gratitude experienced while passing high above some hellish looking section of an inner city neighborhood on an elevated #6 train, smoking stolen cigarettes in the air-conditioned comfort of an empty and sun-blinded subway car rolling lazy for the Bronx.

Shannon
Ketch

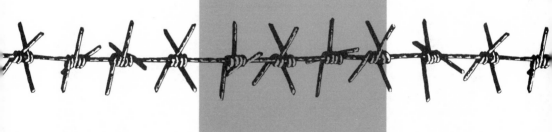

Cantaloupe

I used to write very dense poems
Turning up my collar
Inking my quill pen
And smoking my Chesterfield Kings.
But the one day I entered the mad scientist's
lab coat, picked up a spoon and began to eat his cantaloupe,
I found it very tasty, very sweet, and very dry.
I then discovered I was eating an eraser, instead, and had
erased half my tongue.
Well, note this in your book, doctor,
I was not dreaming.
I was on roller skates for Chrissake.
Look! I still have them on.
The doctor rolls up her sleeves and begins amputating.
I smell burning wood.
Later, this very same day, as I'm walking in the Everglades,
I spot a huge turtle eating a dog.
Now I know, I've entered the world of fine ligature.

Laughter of Gold

All the rain off lead birds
in silver treetops
And victory of sounds emitted
on ponies of glory
From mouths ground down
lower than the salts of mirth
The paralysis of stars
& the funerals of cars

The red coat fur of shattered
early mornings, light barely come up
Ashtray miming the slow
music of angels in crush-velvet chairs
Broken clinks as they hit

night's loose boards
The floor where the ceiling is
but a cracked panorama

All the drains in the house
these tiny palaces
Chirp when victory is in town
that's where I'll be

The Sister's Shade

You were on my mind
like a talking bird on my shoulder
Something rolling down
towards the light conversation
that ceased to exist
An overexposed image
of a place lost to childhood
memories that now seem useless & old
like a tired wheel in the back of your mind
A big hand that came out of nowhere
as you were parachuting into a war zone
that was created under zombie circumstances
on back lots in suburban paradise
where everyone is exactly who they are
Filling the gaps with an inert logic
that rips the couple apart
so that they never give each other hand jobs
in back rooms after putting in 40 hours
at the dump
which is sacred ground
It is the sister's shade
that heals all wounds
inflicted by a testament
to a flaming harry
which is a drink
commonly invented
after hours of adjustment
to the faltering light of this dark room

Beneath Incinerated Beams

Haystack in the shape of a rump
Over a high Ohio ditch
Howl be thy name
Born free
Free as a daisy
Choked by the mind
Yeah!
And send the coach home
To ring some bells with the Mafia
I'm history of all that is mean
I mean nothing but trucks
Big trucks loaded with fruit
Dripping their juices on the highway of life
Truculent sweaty palms greasing up the sky
A brown skull in a white tureen
I say my prayers every night
In order for them to smack me in the face
By the light of day
And aren't they just beautiful?

Uh—Hu

Recently, it was discovered what really happened to Johny Grunt. Johny Grunt was this kid who disappeared in the late seventies at the age of twelve. The first milk-carton campaign to find a missing child was run for him. It was led by his mother. His face was the first to show-up on A & E milk cartons bought in the Midwest. After awhile it appeared on almost every milk carton in America and Greater Europe. In '92, they found out what had really happened to Johny. Early on, his mother had taken him to Arizona and stuffed his body in a deep freeze. Years later, she had become so tired of seeing his face on milk cartons that she went back down to Arizona and pulled him out of the freeze, cut him up, cooked him and ate him. "Later this week I'll surrender to the police."

Joy of Green

When all is said and done
And you say hardly anything gets done
Or nothing is ever done being said
She sits in a blooming field of blathering
Saying what she's saying and it's being said
Rather it's being coughed out in politeness
Doled out in forgiveness
As the crows feet spread out across the silent terrain of his sickled face as
he allows the phrases out of their red cage
Or I should say they evolve like a hundred
Hungry apes out for murder in the middle of the night
Her pearls plan the murders in the mess halls
After the dishwashers have smoked their last cigarettes
All the rain of the heavens vivid in a vision of blue opium
Bulbs with funny hermit faces speaking sportscaster
And death comes early to he who walks the walk
But for she who talks the talk gets shitfaced at local
Dive drinking pint after pint of cool rain water
Turning her skin a warm olive color
He looks at his Timex and trims his mustache
This is not what the Buddha said

Bobby
Miller

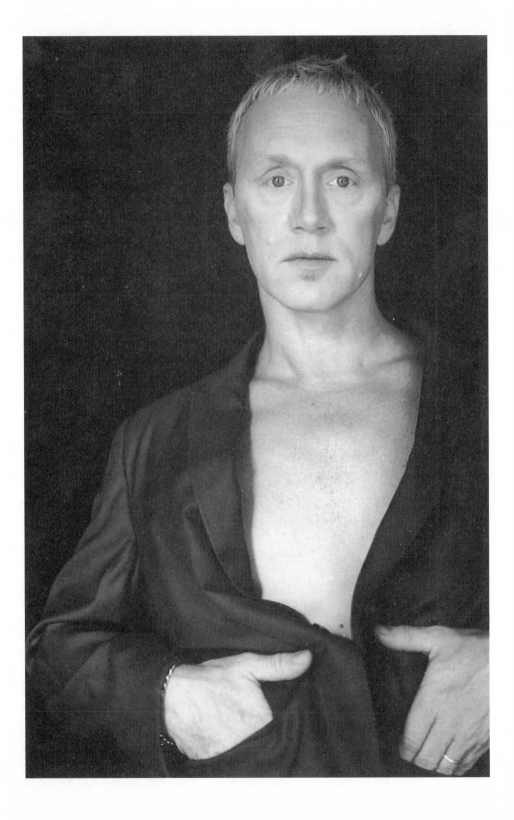

Thirteen

They were two boys
from the neighborhood.

I never knew their names.

A heavyset white trash one
with bug eyes and a fat dick
who stood idly by
while the other,
the one who'd done this before,
showed me how

His long skinny hairless torso
leaning into me.
I could smell him,
then I could taste him.

The moment of first touch
already a memory,
as time sped by into a new rhythm.

Squeeze and pull
squeeze and pull
and jerk it.

"Let me taste it" I said
I already knew how it seemed
or was I simply remembering?

I found the rhythm right quick

"Watch me come.
Watch me come."
Bug eyes squealed

Mr.-know-it-all's hand
on the back of my neck
pushing my head down
towards his groin

Those full hot lips
whispering in my ear,
"Yes.Yes.Yes.Yes."

And then
the taste of come
on salty virgin lips.

Nothing will ever
be the same again.

Memories of 1969

I can feel the cool breeze
of the Potomac
on my neck while walking
up Wisconsin Avenue.

I can hear the laughter
from the pub.
I can smell the dogwoods
in my mind.
Feel the rub
of the times

Taste the long languid boys
with hair down to there,
down to where . . .

Matching Afghan hounds,
bell-bottoms and beads,
love and peace abounds.

Time stood still.

The shrill of war.
The march on the hill.
The opening eye.
The crack of the door.
The voice of the time.

Nineteen sixty-nine

I'm seventeen and high on everything.
The color purple accents everything.
Hot pants and midriff tops,
platforms and bangle bracelets,
blond hair and lip gloss,
top hats and daisys.

The oozy scent of patchouli
oils the air and prepares
the senses for love.

While beautiful boys
like Lally and Ed
both barefoot and lovely
read poems by the armful
till sunrise above.

Tripping on acid
and smoking the boo
Lost in a daydream
of wondering who
we might be.

Nineteen sixty-nine
and I'm seventeen
and the world opens
like a lotus
before my eyes
but now it's the nineties
and we've turned upside down

Back Fence

Anxious moments
spent watching
the front door.

Dinner tucked safely
in the oven.
The table
set in anticipation.

The kids
fed and bathed and bedded.

And now the roar
of his camaro
pulling into the drive
signals the alarm
of possibility.

The possibility
of another beating,
of another heated
argument over nothing.
In a marriage
where nothing
has taken place
with meaning
for too long.

Not since the birth
of the first one,
which was four and a half ago.

Afternoons spent watching soaps
and ironing clothes
and wishing
of other options,
of other choices,
that could have been made.

"You made your bed,
now lie in it . . ."
mama always said.

Half a life spent
hanging over back fences,

Talking children,
talking gossip,
talking Sissy Johnson's new boyfriend,
talking TV.
Talking anything
but a way out of this pain.

Remember the black eye
of Easter last
when he beat you
for forgetting
the egg dye at the 7-Eleven
for the kids.
You had remembered his Marlboros.

Remember the bruised lips
and twisted arms,
the wrenched back,
the sore and aching jaw,
after the first fall,
when it happened
the first time?

He said he was sorry.
That he'd never
do that to you
again ever.

And a week later
he kicked you
up the stairs to bed
and made it all better
with a passionate act
of "lovemaking."

Wanda
Phipps

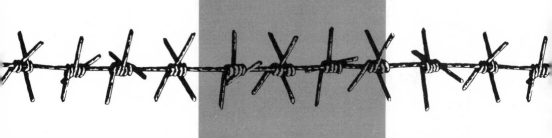

This is an angry poem

I am not a primordial princess
I am not a jazz expert
I am not an exotic adventure
I am not a great tap dancer
I am not an outstanding athlete
I am not a criminal
I am not a sex fiend
I am not the other woman
I am not an inappropriate choice
I am not an embarrassment
I am not a trophy for the radically chic
I am not a radical politico
I am not a crusader
I am not a revolutionary
I am not a southern accent
I am not a nice white boy's fantasy
I am not a rapper
I am not fluent in "Black English"
I am not a symbol of integration
I am not a token anything
I am not your black friend
I am not your black girlfriend
I am not an expert on Harlem
I am not more white than black
I am not assimilated
I am not your secretary
I am not your gateway to Africa
I am not the voice of "Black America"
I am not the other
I am not a threat
I am not a typical anything
I am not the "Black Experience"
I am not to be pitied
I am not to be praised unnecessarily
I am not a decoration
I am not the keeper of ancient wisdom
I am not a part of your mythology
I am one black woman

Zither Mood

1
you said "sometimes lap dancers wear pearls"
you said you'd "give me pearls"
found I was laughing in my sleep last night
don't know what was moving through my sleep
I crave popcorn
"popcorn love" just like the boys
in Miranda Sex Garden
who look so much like girls
what was I thinking
only noticing the flood lights through the window
and a wild fuzziness of sensation
perceptions juggling together
like the two vodka tonics and the sips
of McSorley's Dark in my tummy
I call up these emotions and they set
my neurotransmitters popping
in stereo—no polyrhythmic layering jamming
the system—lower back aching
my boyfriend says from too much Pepsi
affecting my kidneys
why don't I find the Yugoslavian journalist
attractive—why ask why
when a sliver moon smiles down

shapeshifter
(inspired by the introduction to Anne Waldman's IOVIS)

boy/child/trickster
he is one
   he is two
he is three
    innocence/genuine/pure spirit
& mischievous
wild child/jester
he can be many

hold me—enfold me
   wrapping—the word wrapping
comes to mind as in
enraptured
   wrap me in this complex rapture
the moment when
  we are caught up
    drawn up
     taken up
        to split the sky
     divide the heavens
he is shifting forms
clouds/trees
   soft furry creatures
smooth cold stone
relief
transmigration/transmutation
transformation/transfiguration—
a trance in any thing

I look at you
& see my mother's eyes
compassion
caretaker/nurturer/facilitator
compelled to soften rough travel

I look at you
& see my small self
screaming

Gray Fox Woman

I want men to die of longing for me
to think of me day and night
to whine and moan like dogs
I want a kennel of moaning men
chewing anxiously at my bit
because I am so full of sun
so full of morning light
so full . . .
that I just wanna fuck everybody

so what is this?
I feel so happy
so full, so free
it makes me wanna fuck everybody

why can't I do that?
what's wrong with that?
If I can't do that
then what happens to all this energy?

you can only dance so much
you can only sing so much
you can only write so many poems
you can only fuck the same person so much

so what do you do with all that energy
all that rolling on the grass
all that rolling on the grass in the woods energy

I wanna fall down with rolling on the grass women
I want gray fox women
rolling on the grass with me
I wanna ring the red bell for gray fox women
and kennels full of moaning men

to let me know what to do
with all this energy

Mail Poems (excerpt)

1
in
all
her
unattractive
pointing
point taken
came or rather she had
already come
to that
the sticking or rather
thinking point
pointing politely
in front of a taxi

2
hide from the little bear
    with the lover of horses
how you nuzzle my neck
    thinking of her clean shaven pussy
makes me tremble
    jump as the little mound quivers
peace is a mind
    full of juniper trees
       & drunken bees

3
mixing it up in
serious proportions
I stand on the edge
with flowers waiting
for his arms
to open

4
soft hat sways
afterglow purrs
hungry particulars
kick corners

5
tall thin & all
there with 3 German shepherds
2 poodles & a leather hat
a leather clad cat
held in her arms
protected from wind
she was fine & honest

6
kiss my shaved cunt
& bow to its beauty
introduce me to Dangerous
the woman in the spider webbed dress
the wild child filling her mouth
by the newspaper stand

let me watch you
unroll my fishnet stockings slowly
let me wait until you scream
because men *do* make noise when they fuck
but only as a form of worship

Lee
Ranaldo

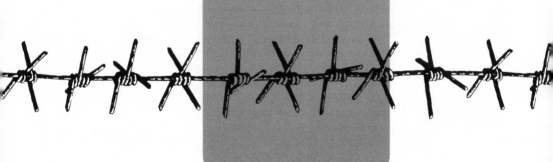

Toronto

Tonight they tore the necklace from my throat
as I leaned offstage into the crowd during Kool Thing
got my watch too
caused me to rip my new trousers
while twirling in the strobing pulse
trying to get somewhere long forgotten
striving to free something nameless
something endless, for awhile
forcing me to hop for them
hot fire coals beneath my feet for them
holding their breath
goading me on
paying my way for things they cannot do themselves
hoping I will fill the empty hole
they feel at the top of their heads
their pointed little heads
trying to be carried away beneath the dome
winged statues watching
screaming for more always more until finally
—finally—
energy shook free, transferred to me
keeping me up all night with jittering boundless visions
they were able to end this day,
satiated
and file out into the cold
maybe leaving with a lover
although mostly children
able to sleep at last.

Enough

Down on the banks
We told tales
Of Julie
A pale beauty
Coiled in mortal sleep
We sat by the grass
You and I in the sand there
We watched the sun rise
We could lean back
And ease her into the river
Points of light on its surface
"I remember," you said
"I remember," and that's enough
To roll up the years
To feel the current pull
To find her honey'd body
Silent in the grass
To watch the dew drip
And see life slipping

Yes we remember
and that's enough
But our past has no future
And her present is a mess
Dark fish swim in the muddy water
Julie's a beauty
Lying in the grass
Playing w her forever hair
Gazing out through the trees
Lying by the shore
A beauty in pale sleep
The earth takes hold
And draws her in

Jasper's Death

foreign coins
dusty silvered keychains
second-grade notebooks
locks w/o keys
pants too small and full of meaning

photo after photo
pictures of a life
pictures of your face
as we knew you

pictures of a room
we shared
when time stood still
for a moment
and ev'ry movement
was a slow caress
in the endless brilliance
of bright afternoon
leaves shaking
eyes shining
hands laughing in the air
quieting the world
—together!—

sharing a slip
down a green grass strip
before the end comes
quickening away

A Bit of Memory

summer's almost on
the diamond days ahead
i can feel it
the need to immerse

to pull under its cover
its foggy haze

i can take it all in
and open the gate
throw sand in the cracks
and watch it filter down

this is the end of the day
these are the times of our lives
talking, hoping
laying in wait
trying to stumble across something sensible.

all the boys tighten their belts and
stick it to each other.
who is on top?
and who is in place?

open the papers
and tell me the news
light up the pages
WAIT for tomorrow
climb down off that truck

Ignition:
charged up
screaming in the din
waiting for nothing
I REMEMBER EVERY WORD YOU SAID
each time we meet
I can't remember
yesterday
but I can remember
ten years ago
when nothing was important
and everything mattered
QUITE A CLEAR PICTURE
the back porch was so significant then
gleaming glasses on sunlit tables
green and gold and brown
you said nothing was important
and everything mattered
epic discussions

150

and then
I'd meet you in the bedroom
sliding across your body
late in the night
while they're talking next door
through thin walls
under low lights
meeting in the bedroom
and not speaking a word

a dead end world
of memory floods
ideas under water
wet as stones
all the machinery rusted
till nothing was left
our house itself raised
I set up a room on yr porch
it was summer by then
the cats slept in the middle of the driveway
the light shot straight through the pines
from Syracuse all the way to Binghamton

a room for me on yr porch
you danced around me in that room
the last time I really had friends
was the last time I really had none
a group without enmity, ended
they tore the house down
and tarred it over

Memory is an epic poem, an endless story, the details shifting in place. Hazy
light on dim faces, photos turning gray. I need a fulcrum to lift each day now,
to elevate need to a burning desire. I remember the pressing need, the longing,
the beautiful empty feeling of wanting, of being incomplete. But that was long
ago. I can't remember how it went. Now nothing matters, and everything, every
damned thing, is important. Memories are forever backing up, mixing up,
jumbled and unclear. All that I have left to strive for, each event these days,
means less and less. And yet every damn thing is so important.

Sunlight Cup *dresden, tennessee*

Spill over into my hole
drag me down
a love song w no love in sight

a drained rain king
fluid slip knot
subterfuge
angry needle-guns
frozen faces
dead roads
bad smells behind closed doors

we keep it all hidden
shut from the light
the attic tomb
the cardboard museum
dust
the sediment of memories
layer on layer

wasp's nest in the secret chamber
paper webbing on the beautiful wood
cobweb heroes
the lies of love

Shut-Up
Shelley

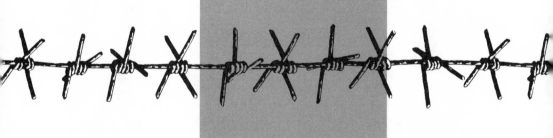

M-16

A POET WHO PERFORMS HER WORK IS
NOTHING WITHOUT A GUN
SHAPED LIKE THE WORD
M-16
SHE BLOWS YOU AWAY
SHE IS IN LEAGUE WITH THE TRUTH
LOUDER THAN A FAT DOLLAR BILL
THE WORD POET IS SOMETIMES TOO
HEAVY
TO DEAL WITH

THIS MARK, RIGHT HERE
IS A DEAD BABY COCKROACH

I RECENTLY HAD MY HEAD EXAMINED
Rx WROTE
I GOT A JAW PROBLEM
A PAIN IN MY MOUTH
TRYING TO TALK TO ME OR
SPELL ME SOMETHING
(But I AM ILLITERATE)
THERE IS A NEED FOR PEOPLE WHO
FIND MEANING IN EVERYTHING.

I AM RELIEVED TO KNOW WHAT
I AM

AND I AM
A POET

BUMP INTO ME.
BE YOURSELVES.

mantra

most days i feel like this

MY LIFE IS SHIT
I HATE MY LIFE
MY LIFE SUCKS

its a mantra

MY LIFE IS SHIT
I HATE MY LIFE
MY LIFE SUCKS

i could be smiling and having a good time
deep down inside i know

MY LIFE IS SHIT
I HATE MY LIFE
MY LIFE SUCKS

its a 50 pound weight of black steel placed on my chest heavy makes my
    breathing funny
i cant breath
its blue yarn strung around my heart and liver around ventricles and organs
    its blood soaking into yarn and drying turning black a coarse yarn like
    raffia or hemp thick hemp rope tightening around organs soaked with
    blood
this is my muse
strangulation and suicide

156

this the side i hide
this is what it feels inside
i feel my heart pounding
it hurts
every time it beats on my chest
it's the stretch of muscle pounding on cavity walls
it's the stretch of muscle escaping
trying to escape
my heart would rather leave
it's the stretch of muscle expressing distaste rage
it's a mantra
boom . . . MY LIFE IS SHIT
boom . . . I HATE MY LIFE
boom . . . MY LIFE SUCKS

boom . . . MY LIFE IS SHIT
boom . . . I HATE MY LIFE
boom . . . MY LIFE SUCKS

boom . . . MY LIFE IS SHIT
boom . . . I HATE MY LIFE
boom . . . MY LIFE SUCKS

sometimes it's just little things
i forget to pay a bill—
—my phone is turned off
i try to pick up something—it keeps dropping
i touch something pretty and it cracks
murphy's law
everything that can go wrong
is already

Almost Making It

Something's tuggin at me
elevator screaming up
a towtruck to heaven
pulling higher
like disco
bad disco
i reign as tall as 3 drag queens
and send ya
send ya
pretty raindrop postcards
from clouds in the sky
little ashen doors are opening
ones i have to crawl through
cramping my insides as i slide under
to a loft bigger than $3000 rent
it's heaven up here
it's taps on my shoes
and pretty pretty raindrops
that catch eyelashes
making me see stars

I'm a virgin fresh wool sweater
i am 20 years not aging
i am screaming no
but going anyhow
i don't care if i end up in a dumpster
eating cat food from tins cause i got no dishes
i don't care
i don't care
about stupid money
or silly photographs on shiny covers
i don't care don't care
about autographs
or bright shiny faces smilin' at me

my eyelashes may fill with tears
but it will look like stars when i open my eyes
i must be crazy
i may be seeing things
but it looks like stars when i open my eyes

Hate Me

It is your right
to hate or love
anyone
you choose
choose me
and my mouth
my strong arms and hands
choose my laugh
but especially my smile
choose to hate
the living being itself
so much deeper
than my personality
which is easy to hate
hate the phrasing
not just my words
i dig the subtlety of hate
maybe a scent you catch
of a complete smell
or gross stink—so big in its obviousness
hate me
its so subtle
when i walk by
i walk by & how would i know
that your stare is not love

fuck art

fuck art
or becoming an artist
or being an artist
or wondering whether anyone is smart enough to say anything about art
fuck the whole idea of deciding anything
selling anything
turning anything i create into something that someone may buy
judging anything
commodifying anything
maybe i'm just a scared little pantywaste of a girl
maybe i'm just afraid and wondering what to do with my life
maybe it is just my life i am deciding here
maybe i am deciding not to put my life in anyone but my own penniless
    hands
i am writing this minute and i don't know why
i don't know anything
i don't know if i would not live without this
are you wasting your time
i know what i am doing right now
and i don't know
me
i don't know who will call me poet or writer or cliche or stupid
or follower or hanger-on or accountant or genius

if the air was something to be earned i would be wondering whether i was
    good enough to
breathe

i share what i create
it is a terror it is a necessity
no matter what, i would be creating something
but here i am so public
i cannot help myself
like breathing and apologizing for using up the air
that someone may need the air more or just plain old breathe better thereby
    truly deserving
air.

Hal
Sirowitz

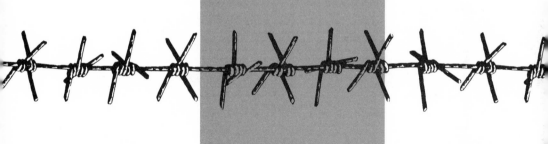

No More Birthdays

Don't swing the umbrella in the store,
Mother said. There are all these glass jars
of spaghetti sauce above your head
that can fall on you, & you can die.
Then you won't be able to go to tonight's party,
or go to the bowling alley tomorrow.
And instead of celebrating your birthday
with soda & cake, we'll have
anniversaries of your death with tea
& crackers. And your father & I won't
be able to eat spaghetti anymore, because
the marinara sauce will remind us of you.

Magnified

My parents got me a magnifying glass
for a present. I went into my room,
pulled down my pants, & made my penis
twice as large. The farther away I held
the magnifying glass, the larger my penis became,
until it was thicker than my arm.
I looked around to see if there was
anything I could do with a gigantic penis,
but had no ideas. I pulled up my pants,
& went to the kitchen where Mother said,
"Do you like your new toy?" I told her that I did,
but wished that the thing I was magnifying
stayed large even after I took the magnifying glass away.
"I wouldn't care for that," she said.
"The house is already messy.
I wouldn't want it to be a bigger mess."

Eyes Are Everywhere

Now that you're getting older, Mother said,
you'll have to wear a jockstrap,
like your father, when you go to the beach.
You might look at a girl leaning over
in her bathing suit, & suddenly get a boner.
You can't always hide it by running into
the ocean, some people can see under water.

For Your Education

This is a tampon, she said.
Since you've never seen one
I'll open it up,
& show you how it works.
You stick it in,
& then you pull it out.
There's not much to it.
Here, you can have it.
Play with it if you like.
I don't want it back.
It's no longer sterile.

Passing Her on the Street

I didn't know whether
she was winking at me
or had dirt in her eye.

Peeping

I once went to this place, he said,
on Forty-second Street. For a quarter
you could peep into this hole.
There was this naked woman,
& every time she bent over
I could see her hemorrhoids.
She probably wasn't aware they were showing.
She had this advanced case.
I wanted to give her some medical advice,
tell her the foods she shouldn't be eating.

Always Giving Commands

She bit my ear, & said, "Fuck me."
But that's what I thought I was doing.

A Question

Is lust a deadly sin
if you commit it by & with yourself,
or does someone else have to be there?

Sparrow

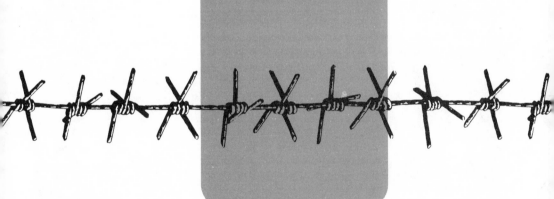

My Sexuality

Yesterday I went to the Duchess Country Fair;
my daughter and I watched cows being milked.
A suction device pulled the milk out of their
udders, and squirted it into big 8
gallon glass containers.
We watched the cows' behinds.
I noticed, for the first time,
that the vaginas of cows are directly below
their assholes.
Every time a cow shits, some of her shit
dribbles over her vagina.

I imagined fucking a cow.
It seemed unsatisfying.
Cows have very few emotions.
I want the animal I am fucking to respond to me.
Fucking a cow would be like fucking a suitcase—
except for the weird thought: "Omigod! I'm fucking a cow!"

In another shed, I saw a sheep's vagina,
as she lay on her back, having her hoofs
trimmed.
Her vagina was large and
human-looking, as I'd been told.
It frightened me—its fragility, its delicateness.
I feared that a sheep might enjoy sex exactly as I do;
that a sheep and I might reach orgasm together.

Cargo

There was cargo
deep in the ship.
It was a gray, heavy
cargo, and I only saw it from
a distance, at night,
by flashlight.

"Our cargo," the captain had
said, laconically.

It was the entire purpose
of our voyage,
yet we never saw it clearly.

And we never spoke of it.
It was a forbidden topic,
like war, and death.

Sometimes we heard it
shifting down below,
as if it were alive,
and we would
turn to one another:

"The cargo." Our mouths would
form those words,
but we would not
speak them.

*

One day we landed in
Algiers, and unloaded the cargo.
But that too was at night,
and I was not on that detail.

Turtle

I have a turtle inside me.
The doctor says it must come out.

If it grows any larger, you will
die, the doctor said.
And turtles *must* grow larger.
As they age, they enlarge.

My turtle's name is Cecile.
I love her very much.

When the turtle is removed,
she will die.

I explained all this to her,
and she said no, the doctor is wrong.

    *

Perhaps the doctor *is* wrong.

Spelling

One must learn to spell correctly
to be a good poet.

I study spelling every day,
as part of my poetry training.

I begin with letters:

a   e   f   g

for example.

When I learn to spell them correctly, I
will eventually go on to
words.

It is embarrassing how often, even at age 41, I
still spell *e* wrong.

I spell it

e

Possible Middle Names of Bill Gates

Irwin
Euclid
Betty
Vashnarawan
Tiny
Open
Heavenly
Toll
Col
Tyrannosaurus
Jed
Mott the Hoople
Buttfucker
Antigone
Pez
Monopoly Capitalist
Orgone Box
Windows '95
"Buzz"
God
Egg Foo Yung
Veal

My Father Was a Snowman, but He Melted

My father was a snowman, but he melted.

All that's left are his eyes—two pieces of coal—
that sit on my kitchen table
and watch me as I walk around the room.

I ate his nose a long time ago.

A True Story

After I masturbated, a
cockroach began to eat
my sperm.

I Am a Great Poet

I have been published in *The New Yorker*.
I am now a Great Poet.
Let all other poets walk in fear of me,
    and tremble.

Spiro

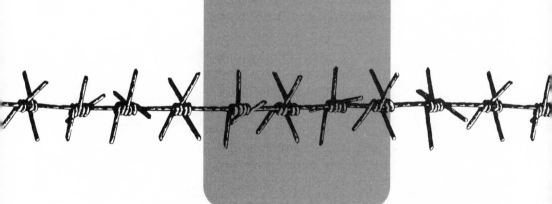

Yet Another Drug Poem

There's this idea floating around
That people use SMACK
Like people use coke
Like it was just another cliché
Well if you enjoy puking, reeling, and breaking into a cold clammy
sweat
Give it a shot, excuse the pun
To be honest
With all the hypertext multimedia online cyber
Infobahn tele communicative interactive digital
Access we have,
To hours and hours of useless and
Insignificant information
Dope does fit into the niche quite nicely
Once you're over the ugly bodily expulsion stage
See if the sixties were about expanding
The nineties are about erasing

So you say you need to be one with your peers
In oblivion.
OK here's what you need to know . . .
Heroine 101
1) Never trust a junkie
2) Your habit is more important than anyone else's problems
3) No one has to know
Sounds easy right
Don't use every day
You use on a three-day cycle for a year
Binging here and there
Till one weekend you go for 5 days without
And you know you're irritable cause you're tired
And the constipation you have, must have been something you ate
And those cramps in your knees are due to humidity
And later your constipation turns into the runs
And your skin is crawling but it must be because you haven't
Cleaned the sheets
And you want to throw up but dry heave instead
So you walk up the corner and score two bags
And BLAM! everything's comfortable again

Oh you thought withdrawal only happened to
JUNKIES

So what the hell you figure
I can maintain this
It's just a lifestyle change
But you're not getting hi anymore.
You're just not getting sick
You do dope to stay well now
So one day you hear, down on tenth street they're
Selling some monster bags
So you forgo your usual guy and buy from some
Seedy tenth street crackhead
What you didn't know was that
Whoever cut this shit was hi at the time and screwed up the ratio
And this is the purest dope your gaunt
Underweight, pathetic little body has ever booted
You used to be frightened of needles

When you wake up in the ambulance
You wonder what your mom will think
You'll need her to pick up the bill cause as usual
You're broke

Things to look forward to while hi

Say good-bye to all your old friends
They wouldn't understand
Say hello to your new roommate who sells your stereo
Your new posture is fashionable
Stooped over, collapsed and shaky
Your new apartment is dark, small,
In a dangerous neighborhood but
Strategically close to where you cop
Your complexion is a pale yellow
You have zits
The methadone they put you on makes you sicker than
Dope
So you figure you'll use both
You get hepatitis
You're broke
Your vein wall collapses and scars your arm
You're broke
You spend the night in jail on possession charges

And someone steals your watch
You're broke
You shoot an air bubble into someone's arm while you're hi and they
die
You're broken
Bathing becomes optional . . .

Let's make a few things clear
There is no such thing as a
SOCIAL HEROINE ADDICT
There is nothing social about it
Nodding off doesn't leave room for conversations
Junkies don't make for lasting friendships
Martyrdom is about self-sacrifice not self-destruction
Needles are not status symbols
Vomit is not glamorous
Suffering is not romantic
Heroine is an ugly excuse for people not to deal

NV

WANT TO
HAVE TO HAVE A
BIG BLOODY BURGER
LOTS OF ONIONS
SERVED ON THE
CONSTITUTION
JUICES AND GREASE STAINING THE
BILL OF RIGHTS
SMOTHER MY FRIES IN
MOLTEN GOLD
AND THROW THEM OUT
AFTER EATING TWO
'CAUSE THAT'S WHAT IT'S ALL ABOUT
IF JUSTICE IS BLIND

MAKE ME A GERMAN SHEPHERD
SEEING AS I WOULD BE
THE SEEING EYE
OF SLEEPING JUDGES

LEADING THEM INTO
GHETTOS AND SEWERS
THE FEWER CLIMBING INTO HOLES
WITH THE HORDE
AND BEING RAPED TILL THEY
GOT IT RIGHT

I'M GOING
TO CLIMB
THE STATUE OF LIBERTY
FROM UNDER HER DRESS
PLANT MY FLAG ON THE PUBES
OF PATRIOTISM
TICKLE THE TITS OF AMERICA

WANNA BE THE
DEMOCRATIC DOM
BLEED IT TILL IT'S THE
UNITED STATES OF ANEMIA
YOU BETTER
LOCK UP YOUR KIDS
JOHN Q. PUBLIC
I'M THE DIRTY OLD HAG WITH
CANDY CRACK PIPE
ON HALLOWEEN
PUT YOUR DAUGHTER IN A
BAG LIKE A PUPPY
AND SELL HER ASS DOWN THE RIVER
MAKE YOUR SON A MOONIE
YOUR GRANDMOTHER A DYKE
YOUR HUSBAND A POSTAL WORKER
SO WHAT THE FUCK YOU LOOKING AT
YOU KNOW WHAT THEY SAY ABOUT EYE
CONTACT DON'T YOU?
I'LL PISS IN THE EYE
OF ANY MAN, WOMAN OR CHILD
WHO WOULD BE BETTER
OFF THAN ME
BY VIRTUE OF BIRTHRIGHT
OOOO, DID I SAY THAT?
YEAH I OWN THAT
IT'S MINE FUCKER
GO AHEAD
GIVE AWAY YOUR DOILIES

AND THOSE SCENTED SOAP BASKETS
LEAVE BURNING SHIT BY
THAT PICKET FENCE AND SPEAR
THE HOLY GHOST TO A PIECE OF
TOAST
GET OUT THE BUTTER AND GO
TO TOWN
'CAUSE THAT'S WHAT IT'S ALL ABOUT
GIVE ME A REASON NOT TO BE
BITTER
AND I'LL SHOW YOU A HOLE
IN OUR CULTURE
IN THE BUDGET
IN THE SKY
IN YOUR HEAD WHEN A COLD
GLOCK IS PRESSED TO YOU IN A
SUBURBAN 7-ELEVEN
AND THEN I'M GONNA LAUGH
'CAUSE I NUKE MY BURRITOS AT
HOME

Report Card

WON'T SIT STILL
These seats suck
WON'T KEEP QUIET
I've got a lot to say
DISRUPTS THE CLASS
I want you to listen
HAS TROUBLE PAYING ATTENTION
You bore me
SHOWS LITTLE RESPECT FOR AUTHORITY
More than you ever showed for me
DOES NOT FINISH WORK ON TIME
I don't like being rushed
DOES NOT FOLLOW DIRECTIONS
I do, just not your directions
RAGGED APPEARANCE
I'm poor you putz
VIOLENT OUTBREAKS
Do you realize what this neighborhood is like?
HAS TROUBLE WORKING WITH OTHERS
I can't help that you've brainwashed them to suck
TRUANCY
You don't want to be here, why should I
DOESN'T PARTICIPATE
You know that old joke about, how does one keep an asshole in suspense?
SIGNED
Epstein's Mother

Edwin
Torres

Power Round

(This is recited using at least three people preferably fifty. You should inhale and exhale throughout the entire poem, sucking air in through your teeth, breathing in and out with every word. This takes a little practice since you don't want to pass out from hyperventilating, but the effect is marvelous. Every person chooses when they want to start the poem and then recites it as a round, over and over, for as long as you all want to . . . the survivor wins the round and has the most power. Feel free to change the order and the speed of the words from round to round. And please, refer to these instructions periodically as this poem is in fact powered by your power.)

BEGIN:

hssssssss . . . oooohh . . . hsssss . . . OH yeah . . .
hssss . . . oooohh, I'm feelin' it . . .
ohhhhh . . . I'm feelin' it, feelin' it . . . hssss . . .
OH yeah-ooohh power . . .

Athenade Booster

I hear things people haven't really said.
It doesn't worry me and I feel privileged
that I doo-n'tun-derstan—D everything . . . but . . . I end up repeating
what someone said . . . BUT . . . . . . they didn't said it.
(silencio mon amour . . .
'cause you don't know what you're talking about!)
CHOY-CHOY-CHOY—NOTHING BUT CHOY!!!!!!

It's a non-sexual thing . . . an original aberration.
It's . . . aboriginal.
An aberration of my hearing . . . but a victory for my heart.

My friends don't talk to me
as *moooch*-ASTHEY*USED*TA/ATHENADE B*OOS*TER . . .
       . . . CAUSTER-NNUNCIATE i front-o-meee . . .
         . . . is like the KISSOFDEATH / *KEECHODEBTS!!!*

Alls I know is Owl's Eye Night!
I-I-love to garble my croutons orgasmic . . .
         CHEEBA CHEEBA WUS WUS!
I-I'd rather smell smell than than Breathe that THAT TONGUE!!!
         NAUGHTY-NATTY-NOTTING—COME!!!

rrrRRRusted Fustilarian festooning on a BBB-R-A-TTT!!!
Pilfering through the morals of a raging CELIBATE!!!

I-I-I LOVE to garble my croutons orgasmic . . .

In Terpsichords of Mother Earth

I could save Mother Earth
if she could only stop falling.
       Tighty-Tight . . . between the layers.
       Tighty-Tight . . . between the layers.
       What's a little friction between friends?

I first noticed the lady . . . eating her cookie-cutter *c?nt* . . .
. . . I MEAN . . . OUTSIDE . . . IT WON'T BE DOING IT . . . I DIDN'T . . .
    PERSISTING . . .
. . . TO DO WITHOUT IT . . . I RAISED MY HEIGHT TO YOUR . . . PAT . . .
. . . CERTAIN . . . SUNK . . . NINER . . . PEOPLE . . . NICE . . .

I could fall in the clicks and pops of animals
if only I weren't so light-headed now.
Depend on the alliance of strangers in tuxedo cloud covers?
I don't think that's possible.

Mother enters.
Tall Amazonia . . . she keeps falling . . . she's turning around a lot.
       Ya gettin' too Hottentot on me.
       Ya gettin' all Hottentottish . . . aren't ya.
       I could cover the earth in spittle-pirals.

Solve another dirt, another dark, another door,
pulled through gravity's insistence.
Sins . . . the middle ones abhor.
Persasicance,
through cloud covered wipey-wipes.

Ratos-Pheroid . . . eat out the coward!
       Sassy can't . . . chow down the gouger.
       Sassy can't . . . chow down the gouger.

One does . . . urinal secrets,
the other erects Hoshi-Monaugural-Statuettes.

       Urinettes . . . 2 volumes full.
       Urinettes . . . 2 volumes.

I first noticed the man . . . smoking his large *d?ck* . . .
. . . I MEAN . . . A ROUND . . . IN ORDER FOR ME TO . . . I DON'T . . .
    PRACTICALLY . . .
. . . DO WITHOUT . . . YOU CAN ALWAYS REPRESENT . . .

       Sally Sins . . . he's the head of madness.
       Sally Sins . . . big crazy head of madness.

A little on the light-headed side, enough at least . . .
to see the bricks [CLOSE-UP] flattened once 4 legged [FX TRUCK ZOOM]
a pixie-tuxedo boy scout in Switzerland, a block of water [CLOSE-UP]
Slavic back to the bone, bare, a cyclist, [SUBTERRANEAN TRIPOD]
another block, another bite . . . the swoosh is gone [PAN ACROSS THE
    CONTINENTS]
. . . CARRY YOUR BURDEN, PIXIE-HUA-HUA!

       Uri-No-No . . . save me the flattener.
       Uri-No-No . . . save me the flattener.

A bugle in funereals crazily bellevollows episodic epitaps.
Little fires . . . the shade will protect you . . . if only I could stop falling.

KET! TLINGLET!
KLAT! TLINGLAT!
Mother Earth pulls me terpsichore in spittle-pirals.
I don't think it's possible to stop . . .

Octavo Piso . . . lymph gnad glyjet.
Octavo Piso . . . lymph gnad glyjet.
A little on the light-headed side.

Steps one twirl, this . . . the anchor to history . . .
feeds me fortunes from my trap . . . sails me diapy-dipe.

Spitoons everyone?
What's a little ocean between friends?

Third Eye in the Forehead

A man tapes an interview with no one
where his voice is the only question
where the music in the restaurant
makes an appearance
d.j. bartender materializes   *so what'll it be?*

A sudden burst into the memory sac
a flow of image from a reading girl
angry at a madman unsure
if her hormones are up to the task
of hanging with his insanity

Sudden flash of white heat
third eye in the forehead in the brain
where the white light is liquid lash
at the temporary public man
in despair of a blank tape

I look up from this writing
the solo interviewer has switched his seat
wonder if he's been switching
back & forth as I've been writing this
how simultaneous

How two events in the world
can occupy the same perimeter
what a cycle of generational origins
loss of clarity - the further removed
one gets from the original - grits   *or homefries?*

188

The Modern Phallus

New Symbol Of Sexuality — Ball
Flanked by two rods / Inversion of expected order
Balls in conjunction with / hard shape = / Context of genitalia

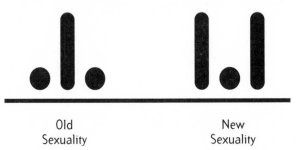

Old
Sexuality

New
Sexuality

Once taken dick out of balls / left with = / Dickless ball
Vice Inverse would be / Infra boom spam & two / mounds
Representing Cheeks / Posterior flesh or breasts / feminine flesh
Two rounds = Testicles / male flesh / Laying vulnerable — to be divided / by
Hard Fact: One hand could cover / Slap one — shape given or shape made
Suggestive of mountains — nature / mother figure . . . lying on her side
Peaks at full / erection / horizon complacent / & ready . . .
inwait . . . inlet . . . islet . . . ninsula . . . penin . . . penile . . . entry / into diary
. . . / valley
Crotch of land gives way to tourists / invading native soil
Virgin flesh / 13 year old discovery / Independence / Suggestive of. . .
New Land / to / Claim / Geometric flesh / Sha Sha Shapeless groinhole
Stake Flag in / Old Sexuality / Unexpected Hot Spot — Ball
In conjunction with / Hard shape =/ Context of genitalia
New Symbol / of Modern Phallus

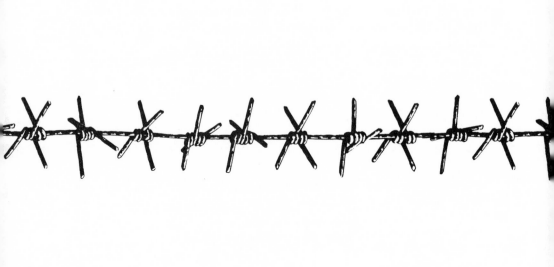

Emily
XYZ

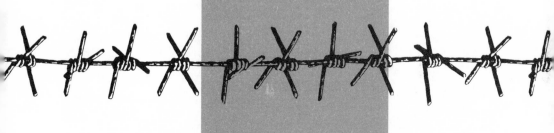

Weatherman

Had I been a bomb builder then instead of a baby
boomer which I was which I am still
I think I woulda climbed over the window sill of one of the buildings you
guys took over the objections of the men in charge I think I woulda been
there with you and not yet realizing where your serious intent was going to
take me I think I would have been one of the ones yelling UP AGAINST THE
WALL MOTHERFUCKER, not really knowing why but sensing the rightness of
it, that the time for this was now,
or maybe I woulda just watched you thinking What a cute guy,
and what a good troublemaker.

If there are two sides to you, this is surely the easier one.
Nobody was blowing up townhouses yet with your blessing, nobody was
smashing monogamy with your help, no one was gagged and tied to your
one-track mind, no bullet yet had the name of a student or a fugitive on it
no bombs in banks, no Brinks truck holdups
the revolution was still clean, just us and them, kind of a family feud
under the April sky.
The administration was dad, the faculty was mom, and you were the kids
you were the kids
Dad you said I'm not asking for the keys to the car, I've got the car and if you
don't knock off the BULLSHIT I'll drive this thing right straight into the
house,
is that what you want?
You got 15 minutes.

Later on we smoked a joint and you wouldn't stop talking about Viet Nam,
you looked tired and disgusted, when the cops came and everyone got
busted your head stayed intact—Far from scaring you or causing you to step
off the sound of nightsticks on backs electrified you, you took note of the
actions of middle-class whites and
militant blacks,
in fact, if anything, you went from warm-bodied boy to cold man over this,
you put the ice into your own blood, Mark Rudd.

The revolution came like a baby before anyone was ready, and there were
deeper thinkers than you but nobody bolder and nobody prettier and
nobody readier to take the heat

Was it June, was it Chicago that convinced you to join hands and jump,
You and the dragon ladies and the macho politicized fuckups?

Here's what I remember: you were the first guy I ever fucked, it was in a
safe house in upstate New York and you were wanted by the FBI, we got
drunk and high and you spent half the night quoting me Che Guevara and
telling me idealism is when you trust your ideas so much you think they're
real just because you have them, and I didn't understand what you were
talking about then,
but I get it now.

When it was time for me to go they blindfolded me and put me in the car
and drove me home. For all I know/you coulda been in the house next
door.

After I got home I shot two bags of dope and listened to the radio in my
parents' kitchen.
At 7:30 my father came downstairs to make breakfast.
Don't tell me you been up all night he said.
All right.
Where the hell have you been?
I wanted to tell him, Dad
I'm in love with a guy who wants to overthrow the government
and as an ex-con you should understand that rage, and you should know
what it's like to be young and insane
but just then the heroin
flooding thru my veins
ceased all speech
and made explanation
completely unimportant,
and my father
and my lover
and felonies
and Che Guevara
became topics
of no concern at all
to me.

Poem for My Brother

If listening to the birds in the ceiling and seeing them
fly across as if this were a barn not a stone
box not a closed book on an endless shelf, if listening to the birds
were not all I am limited to—and if the deep wooden windows
were not the dated panes of an entombed study, and if the sky
were not suspended outside these suspect windows dripping lime and if my
blood activated at knifepoint did not flow like black
coffee, if sea-goats and keystones and swans and acanthus never floated
        never bloomed overhead, then my consciousness were
stilled/finally/and I then safe in a way from words from
memories resurgent right before my eyes,
whose encaséd flood I can
almost
hold in my hand.

Nevermind the evidence, dismiss the landscape
Nothing is taken, nothing created nothing
generated, nothing leaves
the law is not the law
Alive as I am mark me I will suck the metal from your blood and inhale
the dust out of your flesh, that no god can ever return you
to any form but this—
deny my place and wait my turn,
the son cannot be the son cannot be
the father
but over this your parallel
                your axis
                your cancellation
the father has
the father has no power.

Black Hole For Former Members of the Weather Underground

The thing the thinking that takes you to the brink the limit
horizon seen and then not seen thru pot smoke haze a horizon still black by
navy blue sky horizon paces off distance in degrees and senses cut by
crosshairs make the sea/seeable/obscure

The fatigue shirt, the little red book/
the picture of St. Che over a bed that was never mine/that was never made
Road maps in the glove compartment of a beaten-down Chrysler, a little
apartment paid for by supporters of the revolution
        until it is decided you
        are not supporting the revolution
well enough
cut out
target
All the depressing hiding places all the days without/money believing you
were the labor force for some far greater/thing for some power greater
than yourself—
arguing and believing, a case could be made for your otherworldliness
for your stubborness
for your refusal to see what the handwriting on the wall
really said—

And you still have this quality, this belief or whatever/stubborn refusal to see
that you are on
the wrong track whenever you are on
the wrong track
but back then, in those short days
when darkness quickly gained ground it was buy coffee
        buy papers
        buy diapers
        buy dope
and bring them home to your little place to your
assumed name and your alias wife
and act like it was all right
as the red eyes of the sunset surrounded you
and the picture of St. Che over the bed
that you looked at every night before you turned in
never looked back.

brother sister self

wind blows across grass creates silver flicker in green
flashing lights on the runway liftoff flying is
fragile, held up by faith and
machinery on the wind's rough edge I keep myself
to myself today today lasting feel every
movement remember every
word green blue green blue green blue if we drop
now from this height I will die
I would like it but it is not today today river river town town lake
cloverleaf road horizon, where I am
going you won't be now, where you are I can't be I know and still
I am there,
brother sister self
you have located and unlocked and occupied
places where words don't
reach and all things touch that
should not touch, brother, sister
self
using your hands
I reach using your mind
I write using your past
I remember using your breath
I breathe—

4 Girls on 9 Train

these fabulous birds decay so fast/big gold earrings/flat metallic curls/shiny skin/loud voice/long nails striped or shimmering or flecked with star dust/gold-edge teeth these girls are destined to burn bright and hot and go out early/in six years' time perhaps condense to middle-aged childbearing every year or two going w/o thinking of the choices
or the possibilities
birds in a press crush down to fabulous gilt quilt of jungle color moist w/ the glue of internal organs and edged w/ the wet beadwork of tears and sweat and stuck w/ chewing gum to some big machine moving so fast, fast-moving machine made of metal
and men
and time

God don't tell us what to do

God bids us only
Choose—

BIOS

PENNY ARCADE

Penny Arcade, aka Susana Ventura, made her debut at age seventeen with John Vaccaro's explosive Playhouse of the Ridiculous—New York's original rock and roll political theater company. She was a member of "Crazies," the anarchist wing of Yippee and was a teenage superstar for Andy Warhol's Factory. She was featured in the Morrissey/Warhol film "Women in Revolt" and has created experimental theater all over the world. Penny Arcade's sex and censorship show BITCH!DYKE!FAGHAG!WHORE! started out as her solo fellowship audit piece for the National Endowment for the Arts during the Helms-NEA crisis, and had an unprecedented year-long run at New York City's Village Gate. It has also been a two-time commercial and international art festival hit around the world. One of America's most prolific independent artists, her performanceography includes "True Stories," "Invitation to the Beginning of the End of the World," "Based on a True Story," "B!D!F!W!," "La Miseria," "Bad Reputation," "Love, Sex and Sanity," and "Sisi Sings the Blues" (commissioned by the Wienerfest Wochen 1996 Vienna). She is a tireless artist advocate and cofounder of the Jack Smith Archive, with J. Jobnerman. She is a member of Feminists for Free Expression, The National Coalition Against Censorship and Visual Aids—the artist caucus that produces A Day Without Art each 1 December. Having written a new poem each day during her month on the Poemfone (January 1996), the work presented here is "pure poemfone." She dedicates her pages to her muse "Savage" and to John Giorno, creator of performance poetry and the original Poemfone. Says Penny Arcade, "When I was eighteen I didn't want to be *like* John Giorno, I wanted to *be* John Giorno."

TISH BENSON

Tish Benson, Texas-born writer and performer, is now living in New York City. A 1996 New York Foundation for the Arts Playwriting/Screenwriting Fellowship Recipient, she is also the winner of the Nuyorican's 1994 Grand Slam Championship. She has performed her poetry spiced with bluesy storytellin' at The Knitting Factory, while waiting on late trains, at The Kitchen ("also in my girlfriend's kitchens and their livin' rooms"), at SOB's, "on rooftops at the top of my roof," at Fez, Blue Moon Cafe, Woodstock '94, and many no-name juke joints.

NICOLE BLACKMAN

Nicole Blackman writes dark . . . but then New York is a dark city. She's the lyricist/vocalist on The Golden Palominos *Dead Inside*, appears on KMFDM's *Xtort,* and the compilations *Poemfone: New Word Order, Myths: Dreams of the*

World, The Assassins, Swimming in The Dark, A Christmas Gift For You From Zero Hour, Relationships From Hell, Family and *The Indie Rock Blueprint.* She was the November 1994 poet on Poemfone, performed at Lollapalooza 1994, opened for KMFDM's spring 1995 tour, and performed at the 1994 and 1995 CMJ Music Marathons. Blackman was also featured on the MTV radio series *The Man In The Moon,* Spin Radio, Request On-Air. Her poetry appears in *Aloud: Voices From The Nuyorican Poets' Cafe, Revival: Spoken Word From Lollapalooza 94, New York Quarterly, Elle Singapore, Excursus, Tribe, Bust, Cups, Carbon 14,* and *The Fuse.* Her chapbooks *Pretty* and *Sweet* will be followed in 1997 with *Nice.*

DAVID CAMERON

David Cameron is the Middle Weight Champion of the world. He is the editor of *Cocodrilo,* a semiregular broadside of contemporary poetry distributed free to the public, and which can also be found on the World Wide Web. He is the author of *Flurries Of Mail,* a book of false translations of poems from Charles Baudelaire's *Les Fleurs Du Mal.* His work has appeared in numerous journals including *The World* and *O-blek,* and he is the editor of *Caspar Weinberger: The Hot Pants Anthology,* which will never be printed. It used to be that David could be found riding the D train daily out of his hometown of Brooklyn, across the Manhattan Bridge and into the big city, but more and more these days he's just waiting on the platform.

XAVIER CAVAZOS

Xavier Cavazos (Bad Ass) is, among other things, the 1993 Nuyorican Poets Cafe "Fresh Poet" award-winner, the 1994 Washington State Walt Whitman award-winner and the 1995 Nuyorican Poets Cafe Grand Slam champion. He was selected to be in *Norton's Best American Poetry 1996,* but declined to participate due to the lame list of academic poets he would have been included with. "The phone is a book and the book is a phone."

TODD COLBY

Poet, actor, and musician, Todd Colby has performed his poetry on MTV, PBS, and on Canada's Much Music Network. He is currently teaching a writing workshop at The Poetry Project at St. Mark's Church. He is the author of two books from Soft Skull Press: *Ripsnort* (1994) and *Cush* (1995). Most recently he can be heard performing his poetry on the compilation *Poemfone: New Word Order* (Tomato Records). Todd is also the lyricist and lead vocalist for the critically acclaimed band Drunken Boat. Oh, yeah—he's also cofounder of the Poemfone.

MATTHEW COURTNEY

Matthew Courtney was born in Portland, Oregon, in 1959. He arrived in New York City in September of 1983 and immediately immersed himself in poetic activities. He hosted the thunderously popular open mic at ABC No Rio for five years and was instrumental in bringing the spoken-word scene into public view. In 1990 he hosted the forty-minute film *Smokin' Word,* which presented poetry in a form palatable to the MTV generation, and continued to appear in the PBS special *Words in Your Face,* and three MTV productions including *Comicaze, Fightin' Wordz,* and *Unplugged Spoken Word II.* This on-camera exposure led him to a career doing voiceovers and today you can hear his distinct voice behind many a MTV commercial. He has also been seen on PBS's *CityArts,* which features him in action at his current open mic series at Biblios Cafe and Bookstore. These days, Matthew has been exploring more tactile pursuits. He can often be found with a crayon in hand and now when he walks into a bookstore he bypasses the poetry section and heads straight for the books with the pretty, painterly pictures.

M. DOUGHTY

M. Doughty was born in Fort Knox, Kentucky, in 1970. M. Doughty spent most of his childhood following his army officer father around from post to post. While stationed in Germany, young M. Doughty once conspired with his childhood sweetheart, Shayn Furrow, to petition the Armed Forces Network to air *Mork & Mindy.* Years later, in New York, M. Doughty held jobs as a nightclub doorman, record reviewer, and ice-cream truck driver. M. Doughty studied poetry at the New School with Kurt Lamkin and Sekou Sundiata. Currently, M. Doughty sings and plays the electric guitar, simultaneously and in rapid succession, for the band Soul Coughing. This has led indirectly to, among other, more glamorous things, the Indian meal M. Doughty recently shared with Siouxsie Sioux at Haveli, on Second Avenue, in Manhattan. M. Doughty says Relax! Don't do it. M. Doughty currently lives in a moving vehicle.

KATHY EBEL

Kathy Ebel is a first-generation American poet, screenwriter, and Brooklyn girl. She's performed her poetry as a member of The Pussy Poets and as a solo act in many venues. Some of her poems have been published in *Aloud: Voices from the Nuyorican Poets Cafe,* and *Cocodrilo* and *Interview* magazines, and she also can be heard on the poetry compilation *Poemfone: New Word Order.* She was profiled in the MTV documentary film *The Seven Deadly Sins.* Her soap opera scripts have been nominated for Emmy and Writers Guild Awards. She is currently developing a feature film project that she plans to have produced independently in New York City.

ANNE ELLIOTT

Anne Elliott is the author of three books, *Stories Inside a Crawling Skin, Gear,* and *The Glory Hole,* and her poems have appeared in *Aloud: Voices from the Nuyorican Poets Cafe, Excursus Literary Journal, Interview,* and other publications. Elliott is the big cheese of Big Fat Press, and its audio component,

Big Fat Talk. She has chanted, slammed, and tantrumed her poetry to audiences at the Nuyorican, PS122, CMJ Music Marathon, Woodstock '94, the Joseph Papp Public Theater, The Whitney Museum of American Art, St. Mark's Poetry Project, and the Burlington, Vermont, City Hall. Her voice and words are featured on 1996 CD releases *Poemfone: New Word Order* (Tomato Records), *Family Matters: Live from Eureka Joe's* (Tongue'n'Groove), and *Hot Sauce Gizzard's Live Poultry* (Macro Music). Elliott has been a Pussy Poet, an MFA, a Greenpoint/Williamsburg character, and a Wall Street secretary, simultaneously. She will take on any and all projects, and is incapable of saying "no" to work. She is also determined to help bring the ukulele back into vogue.

JANICE ERLBAUM

Janice Erlbaum has a long list of impressive-sounding performance and publication credits including MTV, Lollapalooza, Woodstock '94, *New York Press, Interview, Cosmopolitan,* and *Aloud: Voices from the Nuyorican Poets Cafe,* but none of it has made her especially rich and/or famous. The author of two books, *Girlbaum* and *Girlfriend,* Janice lives in Brooklyn with her cats, Fang and Petunia, and way too much cat hair.

ALLEN GINSBERG

Allen Ginsberg's signal poem, *Howl,* overcame censorship and is now one of the most widely read poems of the century. Crowned Prague May King in 1965, then expelled by the Czech police and simultaneously placed on the FBI's Dangerous Security List, Ginsberg traveled to and taught in the People's Republic of China, the Soviet Union, Scandinavia, and Eastern Europe, where he received Yugoslavia's Struga Poetry Festival's "Golden Wreath" in 1986. He is a member of the American Academy of Arts and Letters and cofounder of the Jack Kerouac School of Disembodied Poetics at the Naropa Institute, the first accredited Buddhist college in the Western world. Now a distinguished professor at Brooklyn College, he was winner of the Harriet Monroe Poetry Award given by the University of Chicago in 1991 and in 1993 he received France's "Chevalier de l'Ordre des Artes et des Lettres." On January 20, 1994, Carnegie Hall premiered the Kronos Quartet poetry music performance of *Howl.* His most recent book, *Selected Poems 1947-1995* (Harper Collins), was published in August 1996.

JOHN GIORNO

The originator of Spoken Word and Performance Poetry, John Giorno is one of the most influential figures in the world of contemporary performance and poetry. He has elevated the poetry reading to a high art form. His most recent book, *You Got To Burn To Shine,* (Serpent's Tail, 1994) collects his intensely rhythmic, sexual, and political poetry. The book also contains shocking and deeply personal memoirs, including the story of his relationship with Andy Warhol (Giorno was the star of Warhol's first film, *Sleep,* 1963); an anonymous sexual encounter with Keith Haring (he and Haring later became good friends); and his thoughts about the Tibetian Buddhist understanding of death in the age of AIDS. John Giorno is a Buddhist in the Nyingmapa tradition of Tibetan Buddhism, practicing meditation for over thirty years. His teacher is H. H. Dudjom Rinpoche, whom Giorno invited to America in 1975. In his two lofts at 222 Bowery, Giorno hosts many great Tibetan lamas who visit New York.

John Giorno founded Giorno Poetry Systems in 1965, innovating the use of technology in creating poems and communicating poetry to audiences. "In 1965," he says, "the idea occurred to me that a poet can connect to an audience using all the entertainments of ordinary life: watching television, listening to albums, and hearing on the telephone." John Giorno created Dial-a-Poem in 1968, innovating the use of the telephone in mass communications. Dial-a-Poem's success gave rise to the Dial-a-something industry. Giorno Poetry Systems has produced forty LPs and CDs, numerous cassettes, videopaks, poetry videos and films, silk-screened poem prints, and performances.

John Giorno also started the AIDS Treatment Project in 1984, helping people with AIDS by giving cash grants for emergency situations: back rent, utilities, food, nursing care, medicine not covered by Medicaid, taxis, whatever is needed. This money is given with love and affection.

JOHN S. HALL

John S. Hall has performed and/or read his work all over the United States, as well as Canada, London, Germany, and Holland. He has recorded seven albums of primarily spoken-word material, mostly as the vocalist and lyricist for the band King Missile and *King Missile* (Dog Fly Religion). His 1992 release, "Happy Hour," spawned the Beavis and ButtHead favorites "Detachable Penis," and "Martin Scorsese." His latest solo album, *The Body Has a Head,* was released in Germany in September of 1996. John is also featured in the PBS special, *The United States of Poetry* and can be heard on the poetry compilation *Poemfone: New Word Order* (Tomato Records). A collection of his work, entitled *Jesus Was Way Cool,* was published by Soft Skull Press in 1996.

BOB HOLMAN

Bob Holman recently produced the PBS series *The United States of Poetry,* edited the accompanying anthology (Abrams), and produced the soundtrack CD (Mouth Almighty/Mercury), where he is a partner in the first poetry CD label. Now he's hard at work on *The World of Poetry,* a combo television-Internet broadcast from Washington Square Films. Coeditor of the American Book Award–winning anthology, *Aloud! Voices from the Nuyorican Poets Cafe,* his most recent book is *The Collect Call of the Wild* (both from Henry Holt). He's got a "Rock'n'Roll Mythology," a "Total Apocalypse Pathology," the most "Posthysterical Poetry," and if he ain't coming at you—he's breezed on by. *The New York Times* says he's a member of Poetry's Pantheon! Wouh wuoah.

CHRISTIAN X. HUNTER

Christian X. Hunter has raced Camel Pro, Pro-Am F2, middle weight super-bikes, and has been an endurance racer with the nationally ranked Reverend Jim Racing Team, as well as photographer for *Penthouse* (under the pseudonym Christian Frey). A professional musician for twenty years, *Cream Magazine* has called him one of "the wickedest slide guitarist this side of Ry Cooder." *The New York Times* has described him as "a vaguely dangerous poet in shades." He is the senior editor of *Sensitive Skin Magazine.* Some of the publications he has written for are: *The Unbearables Anthology, American Book Review, New York Press, The Portable Lower East Side, The World,* and *New Obsessions.* More of his short stories will be included in the forthcoming *Crimes of the Beats* anthology, to be published by Black Ice Books.

SHANNON KETCH

Shannon Ketch grew up in Iowa studying painting and multimedia at the U of I. Contrary to conventions of the Writer's Workshop, he and accomplices committed themselves to writing collaborative poetic art forms fueled by paranormal activities. He relocated to NYC to further these experiments. As coeditor of *Monster Trucks* he internally combusted, regaining consciousness when his gift of love exploded. He performs via the Pomephone and this anthology. Thank you, gods (and 10 South Gilbert)

BOBBY MILLER

Born in Washington, D.C., in 1952, Bobby Miller is a poet and performer who has read at many different venues both in America and abroad. He has written three books of poetry: *Benestrific Blonde, Mouth of Jane,* and *Rigmarole,* and can be heard on several compilations including *Home Alive* (Epic Records). He was included in the Whitney Museum's Beat Happening retrospective and is also represented in the award-winning anthology *Aloud: Voices from the Nuyorican Poets Cafe.* He lives in New York City with his boyfriend, puppeteer Basil Twist, and their little black dog named Smitty.

WANDA PHIPPS

Her poems have appeared in over thirty journals including *Exquisite Corpse, Transfer, Red Tape, The World, Hanging Loose, Sensitive Skin, Long Shot, Agni,* and *Oblēk.* She's performed her work live all over the United States as well as on the CDs *Poemfone: New Word Order* (Tomato Records), and State of the Union (Atavistic) produced by Elliott Sharp. She has also recorded for the audiocassette magazines *We* and *A Sheep On The Bus.* Her work can currently been found in two other anthologies: *The Unbearables* (Autonomedia) and *Valentine* (also on the World Wide Web) and in the new Web literary magazine *$lavery.* Wand coedits the Webzine Big Bridge and has received awards from the New York Foundation for the Arts, *Agni Journal,* the National Theatre Fund, and the New York State Council on the Arts. For three years she coordinated the Monday Night Reading/Performance Series of The Poetry Project at St. Mark's Church and is a founding member and dramaturg of YARA ARTS GROUP (a resident theater company of LaMama E.T.C.). Wanda has also written about performance and experimental theater for *Time Out New York, High Performance, Paper,* and *Cover.* For more info, check out her homepage http://www.users.interport.net/~Wanda. You can also email her at Wanda@interport.net.

LEE RANALDO

Lee Ranaldo is an original member of the group Sonic Youth, formed in 1981 in New York City. His first book, *Road Movies,* with photographs by Leah Singer, was released in September 1994 by Soft Skull Press of NYC. A second book by the pair, entitled *Bookstore,* appeared in 1995 via Hozomeen Press. A full-length spoken word and music CD called *Dirty Window* is set for a fall '97 release.

SHUT-UP SHELLEY

Shut-Up Shelley was the 1995 Queen of the Mermaid Day Parade at Coney Island, host of the Wednesday Night Open Slam at the Nuyorican Poets Cafe, and cohost of the Friday night slams. She was featured in the 1994 and 1995 CMJ Music Festival and at the 1996 Trenton Avant-Garde Festival. She's also been a featured reader at St. Mark's Poetry Project, Columbia University, and the College of Staten Island. She is currently producing her one-woman show, *Shut-Up Shelley Saves the World.*

HAL SIROWITZ

Hal Sirowitz lives in Flushing, NY. *The New York Times* called him "The Unofficial Poet Laureate of Flushing." He's the author of a book of poems *Mother Said* (Crown). *Details* magazine wrote, "These poems map the tangled terrain not just of Hal's family, but of the American Family—its complex relationships, its tristed fares, its desperate dreams." He has been awarded a National Endowment for the Arts Fellowship, has appeared on MTV's *Spoken Word Unplugged* and at the Lollapalooza Festival. He has been featured on PBS's *The United States of Poetry,* CNN, NPR's *All Things Considered* and *Fresh Air.* He can also be heard on the poetry compilation *Poemfone: New Word Order* (Tomato Records).

SPARROW

Sparrow recently ran for president, with the slogan "Forgive All Debts, Free The Slaves." He purchased a stovepipe hat for this purpose. He is also the founder of The East Village Militia, which hands out free books in front of appliance stores, to stop people from buying televisions. He is currently writing a New Age self-help book entitled, *Your Inner Child Is an Artist, Dammit!* He created quite a stir last year when he picketed the *New Yorker* magazine, holding a placard reading, "My Poetry is as bad as yours." His poetry has since appeared in that magazine, as well as *The Quarterly, The New York Times,* and other erudite journals, for some reason, (as well as in *really* good magazines like *Beet, LUNGFULL!,* and *Reptiles of the Mind*). He was also featured in the PBS series *United States of Poetry* and can be heard, along with his legendary band Foamola, on the poetry compilation *Poemfone: New Word Order* (Tomato Records).

SPIRO

Born in Greece, raised in Brooklyn. Spiro, like Bob Dole, refers to himself in the third person when writing his own biographical background. Spiro is the lead trachea for the band Poecide. He's appeared on the side stage of Lollapalooza and was 1995's King of the Coney Island Mermaid Parade. His production squad, Random Acts of Violent Entertainment, has rocked multimedia and performance circuits for the last four years. Spiro was a founding member of Pseudo Interactive and still chills on their web site. You can also catch up with him in the Pseudo forum on Prodigy.

EDWIN TORRES

Edwin Torres recites poetry from tongue to body to earth to the shores of New York City's Lower East Side to the beaches of Australia. A natural-born letter, he's been writing since just a vowel and currently resides in New York City as a full-time syllable, refracting language with baby prisms. He's been awarded The Nuyorican Poets Cafe Fresh Poetry Award, and in 1995 he received a grant from The Foundation For Contemporary Performance Art. For four years, he worked at The St. Mark's Poetry Project, leading a workshop and cocurating a reading series. His poetry has been published in many books and journals including the award-winning anthology *Aloud: Voices from the Nuyorican Poets Cafe* (Henry Holt). He continues to tour across the United States and overseas with a poetry collective called Real Live Poetry performing and giving workshops all over the alphabet. Edwin has two books of poetry available, *I Hear Things People Haven't Really Said* and *Lung Poetry.* He can also be heard on the poetry compilation *Poemfone: New Word Order* (Tomato Records).

EMILY XYZ

Emily XYZ is a poet and recording artist whose two-voice texts intensify the natural rhythms and melody of speech to create the kind of energy usually associated with rock bands or spirited arguments. Since June 1992, together with actress Myers Bartlett, XYZ has performed frequently in New York at venues such as the Kitchen, PS 122, the Nuyorican Poets Cafe, St. Mark's Poetry Project, Jackie 60, and many others. Their performance of XYZ's poem "Slot Machine" was featured in *The United States of Poetry,* a five-part PBS series that aired in February 1996. As part of the performing group the Nuyorican Poets Cafe Live, they have appeared at the Sydney Arts festival in Sydney, Australia (January

1996), the Serious Fun! Festival at Lincoln Center (August 1994), and have toured the Midwest and Canada. Independently, XYZ and Bartlett completed a five-city tour of Germany in November 1994. They have also recorded singles of two of XYZ's most popular performance-poems, "Jimmy Page Loves Lori Maddox" and "Sinatra Walks Out" (with music by Virgil Moorefield) on the well-known indie/alternative label Kill Rock Stars. XYZ's work has been published in two anthologies, *The United States of Poetry* (Abrams: 1996) and *Aloud: Voices from the Nuyorican Poets Cafe* (Holt: 1994), and has appeared in *Verbal Abuse* and *Sensitive Skin* magazines.

CHRISTIAN LANTRY (Photographer)
Christian Lantry grew up on the south side of Chicago and moved to New York City in 1989 to pursue a career in photography. He received a BFA in photography from the School of Visual Arts in 1993. Since then he has been a contributing photographer to several magazines including *TV Guide, Option,* and *Raygun,* and he has shot various CD covers for Polygram, Def Jam, Jive, Elektra, Raucus, Tomato, Cutting, and Freeze records.

Jordan and Amy Trachtenberg

ACKNOWLEDGMENTS

Jordan Trachtenberg would like to thank:

Amy Trachtenberg, my partner in life as well as in this book—she has the patience of a saint and a heart of gold; Todd Colby, my friend, hero, and partner in Poemfone crime; Christian Lantry for contributing his superior photography to this book; all of the poets who helped make the Poemfone great; Rich Masio for introducing me to Dana Albarella, our devoted editor at St. Martin's; Dana "Barbarella" Albarella for having such great taste and proving it by choosing to put this book out; my very own Dream Team of Jonathan (da Money Man) Gassman, Andrew Gelman, Randy Friedberg and Floria Lasky; Ron Burman, my spiritual brother; Adam Vetri for his generous donation of Poemfone equipment and for being a great gin opponent; Kevin Eggers and Anne Amendologine (X2), Peter Hale and Bob Rosenthal; my whole wacky family; and of course, Zelda and Jasmine—without them I would never be covered in cat hair.

Amy Trachtenberg would like to thank:

Bob Holman for always serving up a generous helping of his humor, wisdom, and guidance; Penny Arcade for her friendship and emotional nourishment; Bobby Miller, whose hair and makeup prowess made the prospects of a photo shoot far less terrifying; Glen Craig & Company for the beautiful flowers that helped us to say thank-you in style; Dana Albarella for all of the enthusiasm and hard work that she poured into this project; Dana Cowin for jump-starting my editorial instinct; my entire enormous family for their unending support and love; the Poemfone poets for dazzling me with their work and making the selection process so difficult, yet so easy; and last but not least, to my Big Boy, partner-in-crime, husband, and best man . . . thanks for sharing, thanks for listening, thanks for knowing when to let me be right—together we proved that "office" can mean "bed," eighty-hour workweeks can be fun, and shared passions yield great gems.

Todd Colby would like to thank:

Lisa Colby, Jordy and Amy Trachtenberg, The Poetry Project at St. Mark's Church, and Soft Skull Press.

Christian Lantry would like to thank:

His wife, Pam, for all her love and support; his father and mother and Derek; Amy and Jordy, for their continuous quest to heighten all forms of art; Jeffrey, David, Dominic, Stacy, and Peter; all the poets for trusting his vision.

PERMISSIONS

"Us," and "You Will" by Nicole Blackman appeared in *Pretty* (Spy Verses Spy); "Break" and "Iris" appeared in *Sweet* (Spy Verses Spy); "Rockaway" appeared in *New York Quarterly*. "Twenty Songs for My Unborn Fifth Child" by Todd Colby appeared in *Cush* (Soft Skull Press) and was recorded on *Family Affair* (Tongue'n'Groove Records); "Get Down!," "Cake," and "Seize the Pants" appeared in *Ripsnort* (Soft Skull Press); "Zoom" appeared in *Fog & Swirl* (Evil Clown Books); "The Flue," "Remembering," and "The Secret" appeared in *The Floaters* (Evil Clown Books); "something turned over" by Anne Elliott appeared in *Gear* (Big Fat Press); "Sonnet 25" and "Love Letter to His Dick" by Janice Erlbaum appeared in *Girlfriend* (Girlbomb Press); "fellas" appeared in *Girlbaum* (Unbelievable Alligator Press); "I Am a Victim of Telephone" by Allen Ginsberg was recorded on *Disconnected: The Dial-a-Poem Poets* (Giorno Poetry Systems Institute); "Please Master" was recorded on *Totally Corrupt, The Dial-a-Poem Poets* (Giorno Poetry Systems Institute); "Punk Rock You Big Crybaby" and "Old Pond" were recorded on *The Nova Convention* (Giorno Poetry Systems Institute). "I Am a Victim of Telephone," "Please Master," "Punk Rock Your My Big Crybaby," and "Old Pond" also appeared in *Collected Poems* (Harper Collins) and are reprinted with permission from the publisher. "It's Saturday," "The Evil Children," and "I'm Sorry" by John S. Hall were recorded on *Happy Hour* (Atlantic Records); "To Walk Among The Pigs" was recorded on *Way To Salvation* (Atlantic Records); "How Much Longer?" was recorded on *Real Men* (Shimmy Disk); "Let's Have Sex" was recorded on *King Missile* (Atlantic Records); "To Walk Among the Pigs," "Let's Have Sex," "It's Saturday," "The Evil Children," "How Much Longer?," and "I'm Sorry" all appeared in *Jesus Was Way Cool* (Soft Skull Press). "A Jew In New York" by Bob Holman appeared in *Longshot* (Danny Shot, Nancy Mercado, editors); "No Dream" appeared in *Collect Call of the Wild* (Henry Holt). "Uh-Hu" by Shannon Ketch appeared in *Gathering of the Tribes* under another name. "Thirteen" and "Memories of 1969" by Bobby Miller appeared in *Rigmarole* (IBG Press); "Back Fence" appeared in *Mouth of Jane* (Biblios and IBG Press). "This is an angry poem" by Wanda Phipps appeared in *Longshot* (Vol. 9); "Mail Poems" appeared in *Oblēk Nº12: Writing From the New Coast;* "shapeshifter" appeared in *Living With A White Girl* (no. 1, vol. 1). "No More Birthdays," "Eyes Are Everywhere," "Magnified," and "Always Giving Commands" by Hal Sirowitz appeared in *Mother Said* (Crown) and are reprinted with permission from the publisher; "For Your Education" appeared in *Appearances;* "No More Birthdays" originally appeared in *B City;* "Always Giving Commands" originally appeared in *Vox*. "My Sexuality" and "A True Story" by Sparrow appeared in *Pink Pages;* "My Father Was a Snowman, But He Melted" was recorded with the band Foamola on *Family Affair* (Tongue'n'Groove Records). "Athenade Booster" by Edwin Torres appeared in *I Hear Things People Haven't Really Said.*